What is it they say? 'Two men l
dust and the other saw stars.']
taken from the dust and raised
listen to many stories of God's
reading accounts like these lea
testimonies highlight more thar
where sin did abound, grace does ....
total anonymity of the writers highlights that the real hero is Jesus.
The work of Prison Fellowship Scotland deserves to be celebrated
and supported by a wider audience. This book will lead you tears and
laughter, often within the same page.

DAVID MEREDITH
Mission Director
Free Church of Scotland, Inverness

I first attended Prison Fellowship meetings some twenty-seven years
ago, initially to get out of my cell, and to hopefully be given a cup
of tea and a biscuit (I was not disappointed). At that time, I was on
remand for murder, and all the signs indicated that I would be found
guilty. I was nineteen and facing a life-sentence; the future looked
dark, and life itself looked over. However, I was soon to find that real
life, 'life in abundance' as Jesus calls it, was just about to begin. Life
in abundance came to me in the same manner it has come to millions
throughout the ages, through the gospel. The Bible tells us that the
gospel of Jesus is 'the power of God for the salvation of everyone who
believes' (Rom. 1:16), therefore there is nothing more powerful than
God's gospel. However, for God's gospel to do its work, for God's
dynamite to explode in lives and to bring about a new creation, it must
be shared. Prison Fellowship Scotland workers and volunteers knew
this, and in obedience to the burden God has placed in their hearts for
prisoners, they dared to enter Scottish prisons to set-off the dynamite
of God contained in the gospel. What an encouragement to read in
this book the testimonies of lives redeemed and renewed through the
gospel. Where would these lives be if the good news of Jesus hadn't
come? I dread to think where my own life would be, or how different
things may have turned out, if not for the love and faithfulness of

Prison Fellowship Scotland workers and volunteers who brought Jesus behind bars. As I write these words in a coffee shop in Glasgow, I feel very humbled, and very surprised, to be asked to endorse a book which brings us up to date with the work of Prison Fellowship Scotland. Perhaps someone reading this book will feel 'nudged' to send it to someone in prison, or to the family of a prisoner? Can I encourage you to do this, to take a chance for God? Who knows, you could turn out to be an invaluable link in God's gospel-chain? Who knows, God may well use your simple act of buying and sending a book, to start someone off on a journey with Jesus?

GARRY BROTHERSTON
Minister, Bishopbriggs Free Church, Glasgow

As a Canadian friend of PF Scotland, on several occasions I have seen first-hand the influence and gracious integrity of their work. I have met many like the voices in this book - those in prison, those liberated, volunteers, governors, staff or HM inspectorate. They create a beautiful tapestry of the dignifying and life-changing work of PF Scotland. The voices of the various parties in this book tell a powerful story of God's love and grace and the difference His love and grace make. Listen for yourself and be inspired.

NORM ALLEN
Founder and President of Touchstone Ministries

In a culture where the loudest but not always the best voices are heard, PF Scotland, in *40 Years Behind Bars* has given a platform to voices that really should be heard. During some of my favourite concerts (sharing songs in Prison) I've had the privilege of hearing a few of these voices. I recommend you get yourself a cup of tea, a biscuit and a mustard seed of faith, just like so many PFS meetings and listen in. However, be aware that these voices and stories might just turn your world view upside down, make you thinking differently about faith and restorative justice and perhaps even transform you, just like the stories of Jesus do.

YVONNE LYON
Musician and songwriter

This is an informative book marking the first forty years of the work of Prison Fellowship Scotland. I found it encouraging that a hundred volunteers, two staff and a number of local prayer groups support this ministry to 8,000 prisoners in Scottish prisons. Prisoners are hearing of Christ with some now trusting in Christ. These individuals are helped in various ways. Over 50% of prisoners over the age of fifty receive no visitors; for most prisoners there is isolation, loneliness and an uncertain future. Most of all there is profound spiritual need amongst them. Read this book, pray for this work in Scotland and in forty other countries. Perhaps you could be a volunteer too!

ERYL DAVIES
Research Supervisor, Union School of Theology, Bridgend, Wales

40 YEARS BEHIND BARS

THE INSIDE STORY OF PRISON FELLOWSHIP SCOTLAND

CHRISTIAN
FOCUS

Paperback ISBN 978-1-5271-0778-6
Ebook ISBN   978-1-5271-0854-7

10 9 8 7 6 5 4 3 2 1

Published in 2021
by
Christian Focus Publications Ltd,
Geanies House, Fearn, Ross-shire,
IV20 1TW, Scotland, Great Britain

www.christianfocus.com

Designed by James Amour

Printed by Bell & Bain, Glasgow

CONTENTS

Foreword

The story of Prison Fellowship is the compelling story of God behind bars. In a very real sense, Prison Fellowship was born behind prison bars in the heart of Chuck Colson, the notorious American 'Watergate' prisoner, who discovered the reality of God's redemptive love and transforming power in Jesus Christ among his fellow prisoners. During imprisonment he realised that only God could change the hearts and lives of people, both in and out of prison, for good. What authorities and laws and justice systems and prison regimes could not do, God was doing and He seemed more powerfully present behind prison bars than in the finest churches and cathedrals of the world.

When Chuck Colson completed his sentence, he was planning to pick up the pieces of his life and return to practising law. But that was not to be: God did not let him forget his fellow prisoners and their families. Chuck was drawn back into prison to visit the men he'd left behind, and he realised that God was using the worst experience of his life for good and was giving him a life sentence. So, he began going back to prison as a visitor, taking others with him as a fellowship of friends to reach out, care for, encourage and support their 'brothers' behind bars.

This was the beginning of the Prison Fellowship movement: the story of one man who, when serving time in prison, realised that the God who had given him new life, was real and present, especially behind bars – then returning to prison with groups of his friends from the outside to visit other inmates because God loves and cares for those who are in prison.

Chuck had no intention of venturing beyond the prisons of America. But the remarkable story of Chuck and his friends captured the imagination of people in other countries, who wondered what God might do if they followed his example of creating a 'prison fellowship' of caring friends from the outside reaching out to inmates with the compassion and grace of God.

Scotland was among the very first countries where the idea of 'prison fellowship' took root. In 1983 representatives from fledgling Prison Fellowship groups in Scotland, Northern Ireland and England joined together in hosting a gathering of people from around the world who, like them, had expressed a desire to reach out to those who were alienated and forgotten in prison. More than one hundred and fifty people from forty countries responded and met in Belfast, Northern Ireland to share their ideas and experiences, hear each other's stories, and consider the reconciling power of Jesus Christ. Among them were ex-prisoners like Chuck Colson, judges, prison officials, Members of Parliament, priests and pastors, business people, and many others representing a wide range of cultures, denominations, and ethnic backgrounds. During that gathering, Prison Fellowship International was born; a movement that now encompasses Prison Fellowship groups in more than one hundred and twenty-five countries.

From that beginning Prison Fellowship Scotland and its founding leaders like Louise Purvis, Robin Scott, Angus Creighton, Kenneth Mackenzie and many others have played a leading role in extending, encouraging and inspiring the global Prison Fellowship movement. To this day the example of Prison Fellowship Scotland is a witness to the powerful story of God behind bars – the story of God who became a prisoner in Jesus Christ (arrested – John 18:1-12 and tried – John 18:19-24; 29-37); God, whose Kingdom Jesus described as being evidenced among those who come to visit Him in prison (Matt. 25:35,36). And this is what the people of Prison Fellowship Scotland are doing.

The stories of the people in this book reflect God's redemptive, transforming, and reconciling love behind bars through a unique fellowship of caring men and women from different stations in life, different church affiliations and different backgrounds, who are bound together in the love of Jesus Christ, the prisoner – compelled to care for those who are imprisoned.

RON NIKKEL
President Emeritus
Prison Fellowship International

Introduction

What do you think of the men and women in Scotland's prisons? Lock them up throw away the key? Bad people, who deserve to be locked away? People like me? Part of my community? People who, with support and help, can change? The people Jesus the doctor, came to heal and restore? The outcasts Jesus included?

Prison Fellowship Scotland's answer to that question is, 'There, but for the grace of God, go I!'

People like ourselves who need the Good News, who need grace, mercy, love, forgiveness and reconciliation. People who need to think again about themselves, about their fellow human beings and about God.

So every week we are in Scotland's prisons bringing Jesus' message to men and women in prison, helping the Scottish Prison Service achieve the aim of 'Unlocking potential, transforming lives' and pursuing our own motto 'Bruised but not Broken' (Isa. 42:3).

Who are Prison Fellowship Scotland?

PFS is a charity, which for the last forty years, has been working with men and women in prison throughout Scotland through its family of 100 enthusiastic and dedicated volunteers, supported by two staff organising, facilitating and promoting our work. Those working in the office and local prisons are supported by local prayer groups from Shetland in the north, to Dumfries in the south.

There are approximately 8,000 men, women and young offenders in Scotland's prisons. Every year, Prison Fellowship Scotland provides over 3,500 hours of groups, with, in excess of, 11,000 attendances, providing over 22,000 hours of purposeful activity. This includes our six-week, Restorative Justice / Victim Awareness course, 'Sycamore Tree,' with annual delivery to over 300 participants providing approximately 2,000 hours of purposeful activity.

We operate in every prison under the direction of Chaplains and liaise with the Scottish Prison Service (SPS) Chaplaincy Advisers with whom we have regular meetings and planning. We attend their sessions of volunteer training. The Advisers also encourage people enquiring about volunteering in prison to contact PF Scotland. We share with SPS Chaplaincy Advisers in planning Scotland's Prisoners' Week activities. We also enjoy very supportive co-operation from SPS prison managers and staff.

Below I have outlined the things we do at Prison Fellowship Scotland:

Weekly groups

The declared purpose of the Scottish Prison Service is 'Unlocking potential – transforming lives.' Chaplaincy plays a significant role in this purpose and PFS is privileged to be an important part of that role. Our groups are a little different to most other chaplaincy groups. They are informal and usually of a conversational nature, often with music. People do not need to have faith, or even be interested, to attend – these are open groups. People can come for any reason. We do not mind why they come – it is how they are treated when they get there and what they go away with, that is important.

There was a particular demonstration of our role under the SPS Governor and Chaplaincy in HMP Greenock in 2015. Two women in HMP Greenock asked about baptism and were referred to the Chaplain, who in liaison with the governor, arranged for the women to be baptised at the PFS Group. The Governor helped with the hire of a baptismal tank, and, in the company of Prison Staff, the Chaplaincy Adviser for the Scottish Prison Service, Prison Fellowship volunteers, male and female prisoners, members of the local community, the Visiting Committee and, in particular members of the women's families, the women spoke of their faith to this packed room and were baptised by the Chaplain and a PF volunteer. It was a glorious evening and left a lasting impression on all who attended.

We are thankful for the encouragement of Chaplains, Governors, SPS officers and HMP Inspectorate of Prisons. Dr Andrew Coyle, Emeritus Professor of Prison Studies at the University of London, who was the Governor of HMP Greenock in the early eighties when there was considerable tension and disruption in some of Scotland's prisons, wrote – 'I believe the reason there is relative quiet in HMP Greenock is in part due to the Christian community within the prison.'[1]

'A Time to Write' Letter Writing Project

One of the things that has become increasingly evident, is the level of isolation and loneliness experienced by many of the men and women in Scottish prisons. In a recent survey, over 50 per cent of prisoners aged fifty years and over, in HMP Edinburgh, said that they received no visits.

As a response to this, supported by the Scottish Prison Service, and based on a similar project that has been run successfully by Prison Fellowship England and Wales, PFS has started a monitored Letter Writing scheme known as 'A Time to Write' where volunteers are linked with men and women in Scottish jails who have themselves, through chaplaincy, requested to be part of this programme. Volunteers complete a training programme and then agree to write letters every month to the person in prison they are linked with.

Adventure Holidays for Families affected by imprisonment

When a crime is committed there is a ripple effect of victimhood. Among the victims are the children of those who are imprisoned. People in their neighbourhood know about their parent or carer's imprisonment, teachers and pupils at school also know. It is difficult for a child to deal with these pressures.

We are able, in co-operation with, Scripture Union Scotland, and Circle Scotland, to fund places on summer holidays for the children of men and women in prison and since 2012, over 200 children have had fabulous experiences and opportunities as the quotes below demonstrate.

---

1. *And you visited me*; Edited by Betty McKay and Louise Purvis; Christian Focus (2001)

Below is an indication of the impact on the children, their parents and carers and their support workers. There is much more in Chapter 7 which focuses on our work with families affected by imprisonment.

Comments from a young person:

- 'Everyone was so welcoming and caring at Scripture Union camp. I also really enjoyed the worship part of the camp and "the Road Show" and the talent show too; they were so much fun especially seeing everyone's hidden talents. I loved singing most of the songs we sung at worship … they were so meaningful and got me thinking about God.'

Comments from a parent:

- 'The difference in my boy within a week was absolutely amazing; he came back so out of his shell, he's (coming) forward now….. he will start a conversation with you, he's more sociable even in school his attitude to things have changed and is getting better. I feel like I am really getting to know my son for the first time, and we are having so much fun.'

Comments from a Family Support worker:

- 'All three kids loved it and thought the staff were great – Bill was mentioned quite a lot – it's always good for them to have a positive male role model so thank you Bill!'

Christmas gifts

Christmas can be a stressful time for families, even more so when there is little or no money coming into the home and a parent is in prison. Christmas is meant to be a time of 'Good News and great Joy.' PFS works with SPS Chaplains and Family Liaison Officers to provide gifts for parents in prison to give to their children. This has increased to over 1,100, as individuals and churches give generously, demonstrating practical care and helping to create genuine 'Good News'. Below is one example of what a SPS Chaplain said – and again there is more in Chapter 7!

- 'On behalf of the Chaplaincy, the Family Contact Officer and the whole team here I would like to thank Prison Fellowship Scotland for the extremely generous gift of 209 presents ... the prisoners are grateful to be able to contribute something to their children's Christmas.'

Victim awareness / Restorative justice

Our six-week Sycamore Tree Course, based on the story of Zacchaeus in Luke 19, works with men and women to help explore the effect of crime on victims, their communities and on the perpetrators themselves. There is a strong demand for this course from both men and women in prison, and from prison managers. See Chapter 6 for more details.

Course participants:

- 'I feel the course has helped me look at my offending at great length and understanding what I have to do to combat this, but most of all I have looked at how my offending has affected my victims and the consequences of this.'
- 'The course has made me think of the needs of victims and what can be done to reverse the damage I have caused. It has also shown me that it is possible for me to move on with my life and to do something positive to restore people's trust.'

Governor

- 'I wish ... to emphasise how impressive and indeed humbling I found the experience of listening to the feedback. The last course attracted fifteen and all completed the course. This is a completion rate and group size not replicated anywhere in our accredited programmes.'

Prayer Groups

All of this work is underwritten by PFS prayer groups who meet regularly throughout Scotland; they use news from Facebook, Twitter, PFS website and our newsletters. These groups often include PFS volunteers who work in the various Scottish prisons and are attended by some of the men and women released from prison. We are also supported in prayer by many churches and Christian groups both in and beyond Scotland.

In 2020 as the Covid-19 pandemic impacted the work of PFS and most of our in-prison work had to stop, we felt a new urgency to pray for the prisons and to use the technology available to gather together our volunteers, from every part of Scotland. PFS took this opportunity to launch its online Zoom prayer meeting, which has met every week since the start of the national lockdown in March 2020, except for a short break at Christmas. It allows volunteers from all over the country to join us from their homes and to pray for the men and women held in prison, for the staff who work in the prisons and especially for the chaplaincy teams. Often we will have a chaplain or other guest speakers, from partner organisations, coming to share things we can pray for.

Throughcare

One of the major problems for men and women leaving prison, is having enough support to find their place back in society and to take up the reins of their lives after the regimented structure of prison. This is particularly true for those who want to maintain and grow in their faith.

In Aberdeen, the Lighthouse provides excellent on-going support and activities for those returning to the community from prison and for those at risk in their community. Working with Bethany Christian Trust and Alpha Scotland we were able to help establish Caring for Ex-offenders Scotland – now known as Connect to the Community (C2C), under the Bethany Trust umbrella. This illustrates the importance of various support agencies working together to maximise our effectiveness and the best use of limited resources. We continue to liaise with a wide range of support agencies, including Victim Support, Christianity Explored, Alpha, Positive Prisons, Connect to the Community, Friends of Edinburgh Prison, SU Scotland, Circle Scotland, Clean Sheet, Tough Talk, Faith in Throughcare, Junction 42, Glasgow City Mission, as well as the SPS throughcare officers.[2]

---

2. *Victim Support: www.victimsupport.org.uk;* Christianity Explored: www.christianity explored.org; Alpha: www.alpha.org; Positive Prisons: www.positiveprison.org; Connect to the Community (C2C): www.bethanychristiantrust.com; Friends of Edinburgh

Annual gatherings

Each year in May, we gather as a PF Scotland family, bringing together our volunteers, trustees, supporters, officers, chaplains, SPS Staff, HMP inspectorate, and men and women now out of prison continuing to support the work of PFS. We are regularly joined by the Chaplain and men from the Open Estate, who also often contribute to the programme. It is a time for sharing, celebration and training as well as just the chance to catch up with each other and learn what is happening in other PFS groups.

Office

PFS operates out of our office in Connect House in Glasgow, which we share with other Christian organisations working in care and support services. This arrangement is excellent for combined working.

The Justice system

We make representation, where appropriate, to the Scottish Government about the operation of the justice system. We have offered working PF models of a very different, faith-based approach, both for young offenders and adult prisoners, including invitations to visit these models. We enjoyed encouragement from Justice Secretary, Kenny MacAskill, and continue to make representation to the government on matters of faith and justice.

Student placements

We offer student placements for individuals in training for ministry, education and justice services.

In this introduction, you have heard some of the voices of men and women in prison and of their children. In the following chapters you will be hearing more of their voices! You will also hear the voices of men and women who have been released from prison, as well as the voices of our volunteers, who visit Scotland's prisons every week.

Prison: no website; Scripture Union Scotland: www.suscotland.org.uk; Circle Scotland: info@circle.scot; Clean Sheet: info@cleansheet.org.uk; Tough Talk: admin@tough-talk.com; Faith in Throughcare: info@faithincommunity.scot; Junction 42: www.junction42.org; Glasgow City Mission: www.glasgowcitymission.com

From the Prison service you will hear the voices of chaplains, staff and governors and of HM Inspectors of Prisons. This is not a chronological story. You can choose which order you want to listen to these voices. They all have something important to say.

As you listen to these voices, we hope you will learn something about our prison system and the people held in our prisons. We hope you will see the effects of genuine faith in the process of 'transforming lives.' We hope that you may even consider joining us in this important work ....

This story began in 1993 with the Book *And You Visited Me*[3] and it continues with this book *40 Years Behind Bars* – the inside story of Prison Fellowship Scotland.

---

3. *And You Visited Me*; Edited by Betty McKay and Louise Purvis; Christian Focus (2001).

CHAPTER 1

The Voices of History

Prison Fellowship Scotland (PFS) came into being in 1981 and two of those involved at the very beginning are still involved as Trustees – Louise Purvis and Angus Creighton. They have walked with PFS and those it serves through its entire journey. Here they give a perspective on our vision and the international family and work of which we are a part.

Louise

'Many of you reading this book may not believe in miracles, but to me this book is full of miracles, the greatest miracle of all being the change in men's hearts and minds and lives from self-centred to God-centred. Many of us writing in this book have been set free by such a change. Some however, who are still in prison, are the free–est men and women I know. The vast majority of men and women are still in their various prisons unchanged and to you, I can only say, "You know we'll keep coming – you know we'll keep coming out of love and gratitude for what God has done in our own lives. You know we'll keep coming because prisoners are very much on God's heart and God's agenda. You know we'll keep coming because Jesus's job description for Himself, and His followers, was to bring good news to the poor and proclaim freedom for the prisoners. You know we'll keep coming because Jesus has invited us into prison. You know we'll keep coming because we see the potential for Jesus in every human being. You know we'll keep coming because we have love and compassion for the victims of crime and want to see fewer of them. You know we'll keep coming in our visits and groups and letters and books and most of all in our prayers. And when we come we will come humbly knowing that we too might still be in prison but for the love of God."

We come as children of God, brothers and sisters of Jesus, the whole body of Christ outside prison to the whole body of Christ inside prison. We come with the help and guidance and power of the Holy Spirit dwelling in us. We come on the prayers of thousands of unseen volunteers who are continually tunnelling into prison in prayer. We come with God's love for those we meet inside and are blessed by the love which flows back to us. We come as Jesus's hands and feet and voice and heart to the "least of these His brothers" – and as He promised, we find Jesus Himself serving a life sentence.

We come with the good news that has set so many men and women free. The gospel message we bring is personal. It is practical. It is positive. It is psychologically sound – and it works! There are stories in this book that are living proof of that. All the stories show that God loves us long before we love Him. He loves us before we become good. The Bible says 'while we were still sinners Christ died for us'. What is more, there is nothing we can do to make God love us more or make Him love us less. We can break His heart of course like children who break their parents' hearts, but He loves us anyway. How much love does Jesus have for us? He stretched out His arms on a cross and said, "This much" – and died. We can offer the gospel message to men and women in prison but in the end, the choice is theirs. One thief on the cross next to Jesus rejected Him. The other accepted Him and is still enjoying His company.'

PRISON FELLOWSHIP INTERNATIONAL (PFI)

Prison Fellowship Scotland is part of a worldwide family under the umbrella of Prison Fellowship International. In this chapter Angus Creighton, Prison Fellowship Scotland Trustee and one of the founders of PFS, shares some of the history of the times we have shared and the help we have given and received from PF groups all over the world, from all five continents.

Angus

'I have taken the liberty of slightly amending the following quotation from page ten of our previous Prison Fellowship Scotland book, *And You Visited Me*, in order to give an account of some of the wider international aspects of the work of Prison Fellowship around the world.

> Christ is building His kingdom worldwide with earth's broken things. Men want only the strong, the successful, the victorious, the 'unbroken' in building their kingdom: but God is the God of the unsuccessful, of those who have failed. Heaven is filling with earth's broken lives, and there is no bruised reed that Christ cannot take and restore to glorious blessedness and beauty. J. D. Miller (adapted).

Prison Fellowship International is a reconciling community of restoration for all involved in and affected by crime – prisoners, ex-prisoners, victims and their families; proclaiming and demonstrating the redemptive power and transforming love of Jesus Christ for all people.

The PFI mission is to work with Christians of all denominations to serve Jesus in prisons and in the community and in its advancement of Biblical standards of justice in the criminal justice system.

PFI has enjoyed consultative status, Category II, with the United Nations Economic and Social Council since 1983, and is an active member of the Alliance of Non-Governmental Organisations on Crime Prevention and Criminal Justice.

PFI, through its National bodies, is currently active in 117 countries around the world.

The current focus of PFI is in the following three areas:

1. **Evangelism** – through the 'Prisoners Journey', Evangelism and Discipleship Programme.

2. **Victim Offender Reconciliation** – through the 'Sycamore Tree' Project.

3. **Sponsoring the education and support of children, whose parents are in prison.**'

THE INTERNATIONAL EXPANSION OF PRISON FELLOWSHIP

Belfast – Northern Ireland

The first Prison Fellowship International gathering (we called it a Convocation) of the fellowship groups from around the world took place in Belfast, Northern Ireland, during 23–28 July 1983, with the theme being 'Reconciliation Through Christ.' Six of us went from Scotland as delegates joining participants from thirty-one other countries worldwide.

Held against the backdrop of the volatile Northern Ireland conflict, the Convocation was a demonstration of the reconciling power of Jesus. The delegates represented a variety of cultures, languages, and Christian traditions, all sharing the vision to bring the Good News of Jesus Christ to prisoners, ex-prisoners and their families.

A powerful moment in the convocation was when two former terrorists, from opposing sides of the conflict, Liam and Jimmy, spoke, having been granted parole to attend. Together with the delegates, Liam and Jimmy celebrated in a joint communion service. The conference keynote speaker, Dr John R. W. Stott observed that 'We cannot reconcile ourselves to God if we cannot reconcile ourselves to one another.'[1]

Nairobi – Kenya

The second PFI Convocation was held in Nairobi, Kenya, in 1986 with fifty countries represented, including five delegates from Scotland with the theme being 'God's Unshakeable Kingdom.' The Chairman's address was given by Chuck Colson. Chuck was the man who started Prison Fellowship International back in 1979. He was a Special Counsel to President Richard Nixon and had been imprisoned for his part in the Watergate scandal. When he was in prison, he became a Christian and found huge help in his faith and the time he spent studying the Bible with other men in prison. Colson promised not to forget the men he met in prison when he was released and as a result Prison Fellowship was born!

San Jose – Costa Rica

Prison Fellowship Scotland's first full-time Executive Director, Colin Cuthbert and I, along with over 250 participants, attended the PFI

---

1. John Stott at Prison Fellowship Convocation in Belfast in 1983.

Convocation, held in San Jose, Costa Rica, in June 1989, with the theme being 'Freedom to the Captives.'

A personal highlight for me was when Prison Fellowship Scotland's work was recognised, and I was elected to the PFI Board of Directors. I was taking the place of Sylvia Mary Alison, who founded PF England and Wales, and was co-founder with Chuck Colson of PF International. However, I was not able to attend my first PFI Board Meeting! This was because Ingvald Viken, Chairman of PF Norway, had ruptured his Achilles tendon, and I, as one of the few delegates able to speak Spanish, having been born in Peru, escorted him in the ambulance to the local hospital.

Other Convocations and Councils

Subsequent PFI Convocations took place in Seoul, South Korea, in September 1992; Washington D.C. in August 1995; Sofia, Bulgaria in September 1999, and Toronto, Canada in August 2003, July 2007 and in July 2011 .

Other PFI international gatherings, or International Councils, were convened in Johannesburg, South Africa in September 2001, and in Hong Kong in August 2005 which, a number of us, from UK PFs, were able to attend.

The '9/11' Twin Towers terrorist attacks on New York took place during the Johannesburg International Council. The international flight travel restriction imposed, meant that most of the Washington staff were unable to attend. However, Dr Brian Fraser, the then PF Scotland Executive Director, and I were able to attend. On our arrival at Johannesburg airport, we were met by the Latin American delegates who were delighted to see us and to have, in me, someone who could translate for them. There was a great wave of concern and prayer support for our American colleagues and others who were unable to attend.

PF UK, Republic of Ireland and Channel Islands

By this time the PFI chartered ministries in the UK were PF England and Wales, PF Scotland, PF Northern Ireland, PF Guernsey, and PF Jersey. (In 1983 a group of Catholics and Protestants who shared a concern for prison ministry had come together to establish PF

Republic of Ireland (PF ROI)). We were told that, one evening on leaving Mountjoy Prison, Dublin, after a visit, a PF ROI volunteer could not get into his car, and that prison staff arranged for a prisoner with lock-picking skills to resolve the problem!

Sadly, the PF ROI, PF Guernsey and PF Jersey ministries were eventually disbanded.

Continental Europe

Twenty-four European countries became Affiliated National PF Ministries, and a PFI Regional office in Europe was established in Switzerland, in 2004. It had a full-time European Director and a Regional Service Team (RST) composed of various European PF National Ministry representatives, which I became part of.

Ivan Sotirov the PFI European Director became aware that the Swiss Army was upgrading its medical equipment and transport vehicles. He was able to arrange for this surplus material to be donated to PFI Europe, with the specific purpose of donating it to a number of Eastern European National Ministries whose prisons badly needed such material. As an RST member, I was able to visit a number of these countries, and I recall in particular, visiting the Republic of Georgia where I observed first-hand their lack of medical equipment, met prison medical officers and was able to arrange for Scottish Prison Service medical colleagues to donate medical journals to their Georgian counterparts.

Finland

In June 2006 PFI held a gathering of all the European PF groups in Helsinki, Finland. The guest speaker was the Rev. Dr Andrew McLellan, Her Majesty's Chief Inspector of Prisons for Scotland.

The U.S.S.R.

The first Conference on Christian Prison Ministry held in the USSR took place in Kiev in July 1990 with delegates from various denominations representing eleven of the fifteen Soviet republics, as well as several officials from the Soviet Prison System. The conference participants represented Christian ministry in more than 200 prisons, which is particularly significant when you realise that the prison system had only been open to Christian visitors for less than a year!

PFI President Ron Nikkel, PF England and Wales Executive Director, Peter Chadwick and I, as PF Scotland Board Member, were able to attend, despite difficulty with flights because of an air-traffic controller strike in France.

With two men acting as interpreters, the delegates shared experiences and reported on the work they had begun in the Russian prisons. Some of those in attendance had been imprisoned for their faith, others for criminal offences, and as they shared their experiences, we were both moved and encouraged by their accounts. Delegates also shared their vision for future prison ministry, and their desire to use the opportunities that recent political reforms had made possible, to the full.

Three of the Soviet prison officials present were questioned extensively about problems in the criminal justice system and the treatment of offenders that directly affected the families of prisoners.

During the final day of the Conference, the delegates unanimously elected a national coordinating committee to work towards establishing a Prison Fellowship in the USSR.

Only a year later, in 1991, as the USSR began to break up into its separate republics, PF National Ministries were chartered in both the Ukraine and Russia.

PF Brazil — The APAC Methodology

The Association of Protection and Assistance of the Convicted. 'Amando al Preso, Amaras a Cristo' (Loving the prisoner you will love Christ).

In 1973 Dr Mario Ottoboni founded the APAC programme in the Humaita Prison in Sao Jose Dos Campos in response to the overcrowded and inhumane prison system in the city. He based his approach on two guiding principles: the creation of a loving environment, and teaching individual prisoners how to love and take responsibility for themselves and others.

The APAC system was supported by Dr Silvio Marques Neto, the judge responsible for overseeing the prison and by psychologist Dr Hugo Veronese. With only two paid staff and virtually no financial support from the State, but assisted by 'God Parent' Christian volunteers, the prisoners themselves serving as guards and administrators, the prison operated on trust, forgiveness and redemption.

The security of a prison depends on the hearts and minds of the prisoners ...[2]

This statement by Dr Mario was illustrated twice during my six-week Winston Churchill Memorial Trust Travelling Fellowship visit to the prison in April-May 1993.

Firstly, as I emerged from the customs hall at Guarhulos airport, Sao Paulo, at around 6 am, I was met by two prisoners who had risen at 4 am to prepare for their fifty mile journey to the airport. Because they were dressed casually in civilian clothes, I only knew who my escorts were by the placard they held bearing my name. On the way to the prison in an unmarked car, Luiz, Roberto and I stopped at a roadside café for a break and a 'cafezinho', the small cup of strong black Brazilian coffee.

Secondly, at dusk on the first Sunday, there was a power failure for about two hours and the prison was in complete darkness as we stood in line for tea. Everyone continued to chat and joke with each other while candles were lit in the corridors.

I happened to have arrived at the prison just prior to one of their 'Jornadas', an essential element of the APAC methodology. Consisting of a focussed weekend spiritual programme, held every six months, the 'jornados' are aimed at taking the prisoners through the steps leading to a personal renewal. I watched one particularly tough-looking prisoner, who over the weekend showed clear indications of having undergone a spiritual transformation.

Visitors to the prison are given an escorted tour climaxing in a stop at the fearsome-looking steel door of the ex-maximum security punishment cell, now turned into the prison chapel which has a superscription above the crucifix stating 'Estamos Juntos' ('We Are Together'). The prisoner occupants of a small hospital ward next to the chapel were AIDS patients being cared for by their fellow prisoners.

---

2. Statement made by Mario Ottoboni, founder of the APAC centre in Sao Paolo.

Also remarkable was the prison's medical dispensary which had Class A drugs, whose dispensers were prisoners. Local chemists in the city donated the medicines to the prison.

S. J. Anderson, a female freelance writer in the Washington D.C. area, wrote 'There – beyond those walls – I discovered genuine people with genuine stories of simple grace. And in listening to these people and their stories I discovered something more. I discovered my own story of grace and a heart more open to receiving it.'

The APAC prisoners are known as *'recuperandos'*, a Portuguese word which indicates that the men, (whose average length of sentence is between five to eight years, for offences including murder and sexual assault), are undergoing a process of recuperation – physically, mentally, psychologically, socially, and spiritually. During my final week, a five-man Russian delegation visited the prison and General Saraikin, Deputy Director of the Russian prisons observed that 'seeing is believing.'[3]

With a remarkably low reoffending rate over three years (5 per cent), there is little doubt that the APAC methodology system works!

In 1994 following my Winston Churchill Travelling Fellowship report, both my Social Work Department employers, (I was the Senior Social Worker in Low Moss Prison in Glasgow), and the Scottish Prison Service (SPS,) made it possible for Prison Governor Ken Rennie from Castle Huntly and me to visit the APAC prison to produce a Feasibility Study looking into the possibility of replicating the Methodology in Scotland. On submission of the Study, it was, to our disappointment, decided by the SPS that while the APAC Methodology was deemed successful in the Brazilian culture, it was not feasible for the UK!

The PFI Secretariat in Washington had become aware of APAC, and also knew that George W. Bush, while Governor of Texas, had amended state legislation which enabled faith-based organisations to minister in prisons, as well as in other institutions. This eventually led to USA Prison Fellowship Ministries being able to set up the Innerchange Freedom Initiative (IFI), based on the APAC methodology, in April

---

3. Statement made at the time by General Saraikin, Deputy Director of the Russian prisons.

1997, as a twenty-five inmate Unit in Jester II prison (a 400 bed 'compound' in Houston Texas).

Eventually, this led to three other IFI's operating in Kansas, Iowa, and Minnesota, which I was able to visit and report on for the PFI Secretariat.

During a PFI meeting which I attended in Manila in November 1997, a Research Project concerning the APAC Brazil Methodology was discussed. This led to a series of three APAC Summit Meetings attended by a group from various PFI national ministries interested in the possibilities of replicating the methodology. The first Summit was held in July 1998 in the Humaita prison in San Jose dos Campos, Brazil, which Derek Watt, who was PF Scotland Chairman at the time and an SPS Prison Officer, Bill McGibbon, a PFS Trustee, and I attended. Bill experienced the level of trust in Humaita when some 'Cruzeiro ' Brazilian currency notes fell out of his jeans back pocket and a recuperando walking behind him tapped him on the shoulder and returned the notes. On our way home from Brazil, Bill McGibbon and I visited the PF USA InnerChange Freedom Initiative (IFI) faith-based prison in Houston Texas.

This APAC Summit was followed by two further Summits in Quito, Ecuador, in July 1999; and Concordia and Buenos Aires, in Argentina in June 2000.

The Humaita Prison APAC methodology in Sao Jose dos Campos, Paulo State, later expanded and was adopted in all the adjoining Minas Gerais State prisons. (During our APAC Feasibility study in Humaita Prison, SPS Governor Ken Rennie and I had also been able to visit the Itauna Prison in Minas Gerais before it adopted the APAC methodology.) Today there are forty-nine APAC prisons in Brazil.

The result of the three APAC South American Summits was the introduction of similar APACs in Quito and Guayaquil in Ecuador, Arequipa, Peru, and Entre Rios Argentina.

I was given the opportunity to visit each of these prisons to prepare Site Descriptions in order to provide written material for any PFI National Ministry considering setting up the APAC Methodology in their countries. In Chile, a PF Chaplain was instrumental in setting up an APAC Unit.

PF Singapore

In 2005 and 2006 a small group of us from various PF National ministries were invited to attend a personal training course held for a fortnight each year.

It was a powerful experience when, one Sunday morning, we were invited to join the prisoners at the PF Singapore Faith-based Unit in Cluster A of Singapore Prison for their worship service. During the service, the prisoners asked to wash our feet in line with Jesus' example in John 13:14-15. It was an utterly humbling and moving experience which none of us will forget!

PF Germany – Prisma

Tobias Merckle, one-time personal assistant to Ron Nikkel, (ex-PFI President and CEO), originally worked at a drug rehabilitation centre in the USA. While visiting a prison and meeting with the prisoners, it became clear to him that he should serve prisoners, share the Good News with them, and find an alternative to prison.

His determination and commitment resulted in the Youth Farm Seehaus being opened in November 2003, in Leonberg, near Stuttgart, Baden Wurttemberg State, as a faith-based alternative to prison – a residential programme for fourteen to eighteen year-old male juvenile offenders sentenced to two to three year prison sentences. There was initial scepticism within the justice system and even on Seehaus' advisory board about how successful the venture would be. However, with the backing of the Baden Wurttemberg Minister of Justice, and the support of the local community and police, it was set up in 2004. It has proved to be so successful that it is being replicated elsewhere and the one-time sceptics are now its greatest advocates!

The young men live together with a Christian staff family, one of whom will be a qualified social worker, and their children. The family and the young men, up to a total of four, live together with each young man having his own room. The family and the young men eat together and share social time with the family. The lads take their share of the chores of looking after the home.

Their daily programme starts with jogging at 5.45 am, then education, vocational training, (including carpentry, metalwork, baking, farming), sports, and community service – with the aim of reintegration into their families and community on release. Volunteer godparent couples support the youths, in an aftercare housing unit, if needed. The proximity and support of Mercedes Benz and other large engineering companies nearby are providing career opportunities to the Seehaus 'graduates'. Having been appointed as an International Representative on the 'Kuratorium', the Advisory Board of Seehaus, I have been able to visit Seehaus on a number of occasions and to learn of its expansion to Stormthal in the German state of Saxony.

I have been involved with Prison Fellowship since its beginnings and am still involved in volunteering in HMP Addiewell. It is a privilege to still be a part of working with Christians of all denominations to serve Jesus in prisons, in the community and in the advancement of Biblical standards of justice in the criminal justice system.

CHAPTER 2

Directors' Voices

Since the first full time Executive Director was appointed in 1987, there have seen six people who have filled the role. Each director brings differing emphases which reflect the development of the ministry of PFS.

Colin Cuthbert *1987–1996*

The first full-time Executive Director of Prison Fellowship Scotland, Colin Cuthbert, was a dairy farmer from Orkney.

'I heard Charles Colson, the founder of Prison Fellowship International, when he spoke in St George's Tron Church in Glasgow and was deeply moved by what he said.

After studying at Glasgow Bible College, I was working as a support worker for those with drug problems. Part of my role was to visit clients who were in prison. While visiting HMP Barlinnie in the autumn of 1987 I met Angus Creighton, who was a prison-based Social Worker. Angus told me about his involvement with PFS and that PFS was looking for a full-time worker. A friend of mine, knowing of my interest, also told me about the job. Then again in church the following Sunday, the Bible reading was Isaiah chapter 42 verse 3, the PF motto – "A bruised reed he will not break, a smouldering wick he will not quench".

I felt it significant that all these circumstances had come together. Feeling the call of God, I applied for the post, was interviewed, and appointed! I have very happy memories of spending those first weeks visiting prayer support, and in-prison, groups. I was also privileged to travel to meet the Roman Catholic Bishop, Maurice Taylor, who had previously been Vice-Chair of PFS. Bishop Taylor encouraged me in our emphasis on a non-denominational approach and in the task of communicating with all branches of the Christian community.

I strongly believe in the power of prayer and emphasised how important prayer support and the prayer groups are to underpin all our work.

I left PFS in 2000 and was involved in Prison ministry through another organisation, Christian Prison Ministries and was also appointed as a prison chaplain in the private prison HMP Kilmarnock. In both those roles, I maintained close links with PFS and facilitated both PFS Bible study groups and Sycamore Tree courses in HMP Kilmarnock.'

Many men, in and out of prison, have very fond memories of Colin, his warmth, the compassion he showed and the practical help he gave them.

Allan Grant *1994–2000*

'In 1994 my wife and I were returning to the UK from Japan. We had been with the missionary organisation Operation Mobilisation and were praying about our future. When a PFS Trustee and friend, Neill Fraser, knew of our return to Scotland he challenged me to join PFS. Taking this up at the end of 1994 I felt was a big step. Transitioning from overseas missions to the world of prisoners and their families in Scotland was a big change.

My fears were quickly dispelled once I got to know Colin Cuthbert, the trustees and the volunteers. Colin and I worked together for two years before he left. It was amazing then how he and the trustees had built up a network of forty committed prayer groups and almost 200 volunteers sharing in sixteen prisons throughout Scotland. Many of these people were a huge support to me in what was a steep learning curve. The commitment and zeal of everyone involved was inspiring. Sharing along with volunteers the Good News of Jesus and His kingdom with inmates throughout most of Scotland's jails was a privilege. Also getting to know some ex-offenders after their release and their struggles.

The work was strongly underpinned by prayer, reflecting the spiritual battle. A number of those deeply committed were not anywhere near jails. It was special to visit the Tiree prayer group! One memory of practical help to prisoners' families was the Angel Tree initiative. It was very moving to distribute Christmas presents on behalf of prisoners.

During my five and a half years with PFS our base most of the time was in Ellesmere St, Glasgow in what was once a church. It provided plenty of room for the office and also meetings. The weekly drop-in on Thursdays for ex-offenders and their families also took place there, ably led by trustee Denis Bovey and his wife Anne. It was a great time for fellowship and encouragement of partners of those in jail and nurturing those newly released from jail. This drop-in concept was further extended to cover other cities as Eddie Murison and other staff came on board.

With regular meetings in nearly all the Scottish prisons there was a constant need for training of volunteers. This was in equipping people both for ministry to prisoners as well as complying with prison regulations. The annual conference and training weekends were a great opportunity for the PF teams and prayer groups scattered throughout Scotland to worship, celebrate and learn together.

All the Trustees led by Kenneth Mackenzie were very supportive. I was grateful for their expertise and collective wisdom, and their personal encouragement. Angus Creighton was a faithful mentor and prayer support throughout my time and indeed for many years afterwards. One memory was the creation and implementation of a three year strategic plan based on Isaiah chapter 61 verses 1- 3.

On the international front it was great to represent Scotland in several PF International Convocations and experience the breadth of the PF family worldwide. It was also a privilege to be involved in a small way in the design of the Sycamore Tree Project before it was rolled out to various countries.

When I left my lingering memory was of having worked with a special family faithfully committed to bringing the light of Jesus to prisoners and not giving up on people. To continually find, as is so often said, that Jesus was already in our jails and that HE is at work bringing 'bruised reeds' into the kingdom.'

Brian Fraser *2000–2010*

After almost twenty years of growth and development, PFS entered the new Millennium facing a number of challenges in its management and organisation. The work carried out in Scotland's prisons by a wide range of volunteers over the previous two decades continued apace, but issues confronted the Fellowship as to how best to harness, develop and promote its much needed faith-based ministry across the country, not only to the range of prisons and inmates, but also to the various agencies with whom we had to meaningfully engage. These were the challenges faced by PFS new Executive Director Brian Fraser.

'In the summer of 2000 when I joined PFS, a lot was going on and it was encouraging to see all the ministry happening among the men and women in prison, but quite quickly I could see that some key challenges were facing us as an organisation. At that time the things that were uppermost in my mind and that of the board were:

- How do we secure an adequate home and facilities for PFS?
- How can we organise and develop volunteer groups and pro-grammes to give greater relevant coverage?
- How do we secure increased resources for the work?
- How should we more fruitfully engage with prison chaplaincy, local and national, across the spectrum?
- How might we engage meaningfully with the various church denominations to promote the ministry and recruit to it?
- How could we work effectively with the Scottish Prison Service to ensure recognition and acceptability?

The faith, time, commitment, and expertise of the PFS Board and its dedicated Field Officers, Terry Paterson, Derek Watt and Billy Paul, were to prove critical and enabled our small management team to help support the wider group of volunteers at the 'chalk face' to accomplish our mission.

At the very beginning of this new decade in 2000, we settled into excellent new premises at the International Christian College (ICC), close to the centre of Glasgow. With space, parking and use of the

College facilities, the administration of PFS was improved and made more available to the wider ministry, with training and conference space and input at times from ICC staff and students. Not least, we were greatly encouraged and assisted by the College Principal, Tony Sargent, in the promotion of our work. In the Prison Fellowship office I was aided by skilled administrative staff, firstly with Terry, then Eleanor and latterly by the redoubtable Anne Wilson!

One of our priorities at this time was to have a more comprehensive approach to volunteer training and consistency in the methodologies and approaches used by the various prison groups. Sterling work by Terry Paterson and colleagues at this time brought a fresh approach on what to do/not to do and how to best organise and deliver the 'message' that make the PFS time in prison an even more meaningful part of the week. Mistakes in presentations were minimised and some questionable assertions dealt with! (I, myself, recall being taken to task by a seasoned and sceptical chaplain when emphasising our role in taking Christ into the prison – his justifiable retort was 'Why? He's already here!'

During this time PF Scotland's enthusiastic involvement in the Global Prison Fellowship ministry brought about the introduction of Prison Fellowship International's recommended programme, the Sycamore Tree Course, focussing on victim awareness and restorative justice. This successful and long-running series of courses has contributed to so many changed lives.

Our active involvement in the work of Prison Fellowship International during this was also useful in keeping abreast of new ideas and programmes. The work of Angus Creighton, on the International Board globally and in Europe as a key member of the Regional Service Team (RST), was a significant benefit to the ministry internationally and to our own ministries in Scotland, England & Wales and Northern Ireland. The close coordination of the UK ministries is very much due to the encouragement of Angus and Robin Scott in Belfast, as in earlier years was that of Sylvia Mary Alison and our own Louise Purvis. (It has been said that these inputs have seen PF Scotland consistently 'punching above its weight' on the international development of the global PF ministry).

A side effect of looking beyond our own shores was the bringing of wider PF concepts to our work here in Scotland. Angus Creighton and I used Winston Churchill fellowships in this way – Angus with APAC (Association of Protection and Assistance of the Convicted) in Brazil and IFI (Inner Freedom Initiative) in USA methodologies (detailed elsewhere in this book) and myself with Restorative Justice innovations from the USA and New Zealand.

Our aim to increase and expand the in-prison volunteer groups was accompanied by an emphasis on prayer groups as a key part of the PF mission. Organised prayer activity within the volunteer group attached to a prison was also accompanied by regional prayer groups outwith a prison catchment area. One such committed group was that on the island of Tiree, which I had the privilege of visiting. This was a quite unique group – the farming community could not always meet together, but were able to engage by telephone across the island at specific times. My quick visit lasted three days due to poor weather cancelling the daily flight. Probably the longest prayer meeting of the decade! But made memorable by the fine hospitality of the PF stalwart MacDonald family at their farm.

Another priority was the continuous challenge of funding the work. The generous support of donors such as Brian Souter, Donald MacDonald and Tom Farmer provided the scope for expansion and development. Other support, such as the provision of vehicles (thanks to Vardy and Murchison Groups), made life easier and travel throughout the country by Field Officers more possible.

The importance of support for PFS across the broad denominational spectrum of churches in Scotland was appreciated by the PFS Board and engagement with church leaders helped to spread the word. The former Moderator of the Church of Scotland, the Rev. Andrew McLellan, had become Chief Inspector of Prisons and attended, with Angus Creighton and myself, the European Regional Caucus in Finland in 2006 as a keynote speaker. Our PFI colleagues in Washington and our fellow Europeans expressed amazement (and not a little envy!) of Scotland having as Chief Inspector of Prisons a leader of the national church.

In the same year, current Scottish Church leaders, the Rev. Jim Gibson and the Rev. David Cameron visited the PF Europe headquarters in Lausanne as guests of European Director Ivan Sotirov, to learn more about the work of Prison Fellowship. PFS Executive Director accompanied these influential church leaders and continued this growing relationship.

The way in which the work of PFS was being promoted in this sphere assisted in bringing knowledge of the ministry to a wider audience, with the oft-stated aim of generating 1) prayer support 2) personal support and 3) funding support (in that order!). This was seen to be happening when the Church of Scotland Guild appointed PFS as one of its charitable partners (from a long list of applicants) over a three year period. This resulted in much very worthwhile work for the Field Officers, touring the country to speak to Guilds – and meeting the aims above, with significant prayer and funding support and, indeed, an interest in volunteering.

The Board of Trustees were delighted at this time to secure the appointment of David McEwan of Edinburgh as a Trustee and PFS Treasurer, bringing an excellent professional, focussed and innovative approach to our finances. Various presentations, hosted by the McDonalds, were fruitful in this sphere.

Good working arrangements with prison chaplains locally were essential to the outreach with prisoners and during this decade the Field Officers strengthened their local links. At the same time, Terry and I also joined a working group with the National Chaplaincy Advisers at Scottish Prison Service. Regular meetings at SPS headquarters helped defuse any specific issues which might cause difficulty in local prisons. Working with senior officials at SPS, a risk assessment procedure was devised to allow former prisoners to enrol as PFS volunteers and the new training sessions for volunteers benefited from direct SPS input. The invitation by SPS for me as Executive Director to take a place on the National Chaplaincy Board was evidence of a growing relationship and provided a useful opportunity for networking and promoting PFS with other agencies.

In the political sphere, it was encouraging to meet with prominent Scottish figures wishing to know more about our work. Following interesting meetings with MPs such as Annabelle Goldie and Mohammad Sarwar, we were delighted to sit down with the Scottish

Justice Minister, Kenney MacAskill, to inform him of our work particularly with female prisoners in which he had a strong interest. It was reassuring to hear at first hand that the Minister and his Government had no issues whatsoever with a growing faith-based PF ministry within the prison system

These various strands of management activity in this first decade of the new millennium were very much "behind the scenes", while the really vital work of committed volunteers reaching out to prisoners with the message of the Good News on a daily basis is what Prison Fellowship is about. However, if the work of the Board of Trustees and its staff can help facilitate the delivery of Prison Fellowship's aims, then we can say that the proclamation of Chuck Colson some thirty years ago has held true:

> *The Spirit's inexorable power is not confined*
> *to compelling individual men and women;*
> *he also calls into being, powerful movements*
> *throughout history ... nowhere is this more*
> *evident than in Prison Fellowship Scotland.*'

Billy Paul *2011–2016*

'I have been a volunteer for PFS since 1981 and when I retired from work in Education, in 2008, I volunteered with the PFS groups, working in HMP Barlinnie, HMP Greenock and HMP Kilmarnock, and saw first-hand and valued more of PF's work and volunteers. The position of Executive Director became vacant in 2010, I applied and in January 2011, I was delighted to be appointed. I served until 2016. During this time, I had the opportunity to visit all the PFS groups and to speak with the chaplains and governors.

With the Trustees, we felt it was important to foster the PF family bond on two fronts. On the one hand, with our volunteers, by establishing an Annual Gathering, and also to get together annually with our sister organisations PF England and Wales, and PF Northern Ireland. Because Prison Fellowship International is a worldwide family, at our Annual Gatherings as well as representatives of the UK PF family, we enjoyed the company of members of PF International

– Ron Nikkel, President; Norm Allen, Touchstone Ministries and Dominique Alexandre European Director, attended our annual Gatherings. Other members of the PFI worldwide family visited us at other times. We also were able to visit and learn from the work of other PF groups in Europe. Angus Creighton has spoken about some of this in the previous chapter.

I have written elsewhere in the book about my work with PFS and will not elaborate here. However, one of the happiest initiatives we were able to establish was a programme to work with Circle Scotland and SU Scotland in providing adventure holidays for the children of men and women in prison, where the children could be themselves with other young people, no other children needing to know about their family circumstances.

The time I spent as Executive Director, was very special for me and I know the other Directors, who have had this role, would agree about the privilege it is to work, as part of Chaplaincy, on behalf of men and women in prison and their families. Our work to recruit and train volunteers and promote our work within the SPS and with our supporters has been a privilege and I am grateful.'

Terry Paterson *2016–2019*

'My own faith journey began in 1991 because of the testimony of one man who had become a Christian whilst serving his last prison sentence. He shared how volunteers from Prison Fellowship had encouraged him to read and ask questions about faith and the Bible; how they supported him on release and helped him find a supportive church in his home town. He spoke with complete confidence that the God who saved him in his time of desperation could do the same for me and my household. I thank the Lord for Michael's boldness on the evening of January 6th, 1991 in sharing how God had changed him from a criminal to a child of the King and that He could do the same for me.

I also thank the Lord for Michael introducing me to the ministry of PF Scotland where I had the privilege of sharing my faith for twenty-five years. Sharing with men and women who were facing challenging times and using Scripture to bring some comfort to them that God loved them, and He would forgive them if they asked Him into their life. Today I have good friends who I have coffee and chats with that I first met in those early days at Fellowship groups in Greenock prison when they were serving sentences. It is such an encouragement to see people, who were once judged as a waste of time by society, now valued members of local communities and churches, and serving the Lord.

One of the great privileges I had was delivering 'The Sycamore Tree Course' for sixteen years. This is a Restorative Justice/Victim Awareness course run over six sessions by Prison Fellowship groups around the world. The course, based on the story of Zacchaeus in Luke 19:1-10, challenges both presenter and participants to investigate what *Restorative Justice* looks like; looking at *Taking Responsibility for our actions*, encouraging us to *Say Sorry and Act Sorry*; understanding what *Reconciliation* would mean in our lives and *Take the Next Step* by writing a new tomorrow for ourselves. These statements are easy to write down and say but, as demand increased for the course to be delivered, I found that it unexpectedly plumbed depths in my own life by repeatedly experiencing the effect that the participants face up to during their course. I found that every time I presented the course, I was being challenged to understand what I needed to change in my life, enabling me to relate my own life experiences during the sessions, which helped the participants to open up about themselves, building good rapport over our time together. Sycamore was for everyone's benefit, not just those serving a sentence.

The course recruitment process was open to all, without any necessity to have an understanding of faith, God or Christianity. Many who attended would never have anything to do with the chaplaincy departments in the prison normally, but were happy to come along as it was a faith-based, but not faith-promoting course. This, of course, being acceptable we then were very careful not to breach their trust. Some may say this was not the right approach, but because we respected that boundary the questions regarding faith flowed naturally from the men and women participating. During the tea and coffee breaks my story of how Christ had changed my life was a common conversation, with many later joining the Fellowship groups in the prison to ask their questions and find out more.

The journey of Sycamore in Scotland started in 2002 with the first courses delivered in Polmont Young Offenders Institution and the original Low Moss prison in Bishopbriggs. The early days were as much about us, as presenters, finding our own way of working with the material, as it was delivering a challenge to those attending the course to think through how their life choices and offences had affected others, including the effects on their own family members and loved ones. Even in those days, the Lord was good to us, allowing us to hear good feedback from participants at the end of the course and from staff and governors who regularly sat through the weekly sessions.

I often remember a then teenager called Graham. Graham was doing a four-year sentence for assault to severe injury and permanent disfigurement. As one of five young men on that particular course, Graham was the only one who wrestled with the fact that he had damaged another person to such an extent that the young victim required twenty-four hour support for the rest of his life. Once the course was finished, he joined us at the regular Prison Fellowship group where we studied the Bible, helped the men to understand Scripture and encouraged them to read their Bibles and consider a life with Christ. A short time later Graham, with great gusto, informed us that he had spoken to his lawyer and asked if he could write a letter of apology to his victim and the victim's family. The reason he asked for this was that during the Sycamore course he realised that only he could answer the question – common among victims – 'Why me?' He wanted the opportunity to explain himself. Of course, this was denied, but he persisted until the authorities realised he was genuine and wanted to explain his actions and apologise to the family. For the next eighteen months, he worked hard with officials, who checked and double-checked his motives and eventually they supported him allowing the letter to be sent to his victim's lawyer. Unfortunately for Graham, the family rejected his approach and that was the end of the road. 'Was this a waste of time?' I asked myself. I don't believe so; Graham left prison a stronger young man, who had examined his actions and motives as a result of taking responsibility for his bad choices in life and was determined not to continue a life of crime.

As demand for Sycamore increased, it was necessary to train more volunteers to deliver the course material. Opportunities opened up in other prisons: Aberdeen, Inverness, Perth, Glenochil, Shotts, Barlinnie, the new Low Moss, Greenock, Kilmarnock and Castle Huntly Open Estate. For the next few years, I spent many an hour in my car, driving from one location to another, facilitating training sessions and recruiting new volunteers. This was a great privilege for me as I met and spent time with the most enthusiastic people who all caught the vision of Sycamore for themselves. On the long drives home, I often reflected on the conversation Paul had with King Agrippa where Paul, in Acts 26:29, said, 'Short time or long – I pray to God that not only you but all who are listening to me today may become what I am, except for these chains'. In the same way, Paul desired that for Agrippa, I would pray the same for each person I had interacted with that day, whether prisoner or staff, that they would see and accept Christ for themselves.

I loved reflecting also on verse 10 of Luke 19, which says 'For the Son of Man came to seek and to save the lost', as this was exactly what we wanted to see happen during the Sycamore courses; to see many people set free from the guilt and shame they carried for years and dare to believe that they were not a lost cause and that they could have a future free from offending.

It is a pleasure and a privilege to be called a child of God, to witness daily for Him and to see lives changed for Christ. To think this all came about in my life because of Prison Fellowship volunteers being faithful in serving a man called Michael in prison in the 1980s, with the Gospel message that changed his life. God is good!'

The current Executive Director of Prison Fellowship Scotland, John Nonhebel, will be the voice of the concluding chapter of this book.

CHAPTER 3

Women's Voices

In the next two chapters you will hear the voices of some of the people we serve in Scotland's prisons. All are welcomed and no one is turned away. They bring their own histories, often of chaotic lifestyles as you will see, but they are the true stories of real people, the kind of people Prison Fellowship volunteers meet with each week.

In this chapter women will tell you about themselves in their own way and in their own words. They are still serving their sentences. Some aspects of their stories may shock or disturb you but you will also see that, despite their history and difficulties, they have found strength and real change as a result of their faith and the support they have received on their journeys of faith. Their identity has been protected by only using the first letter of their names.

A. 'When I was remanded in custody for the first time, I was out of my comfort zone. I struggled to interact with other prisoners initially and found it hard to adapt to prison routine and life. One of the prisoners suggested I go along to Prison Fellowship, which is run by Prison Fellowship volunteers. I wasn't sure what to expect and whether I'd be welcome as I hadn't been to church in a long time and felt, after doing wrong, I wouldn't be welcome. Almost instantly I felt welcome and part of the group. I quickly realised that everyone sins and that when I was ready to ask for God's forgiveness I could. Over the last five months I have sought to do so. I now look forward to Prison Fellowship on Sunday morning, Sunday afternoon and Wednesday evening. Not only do we get the chance to escape from the prison routine but leave feeling upbeat and hopeful that we are forgiven by God and we can continue to rebuild our lives.

I think the volunteers and the Bible studies we carry out have not only helped me through my sentence but have also allowed me to change my thinking and ask for forgiveness, which has allowed me to rebuild my relationships with my family and friends. Prison Fellowship for many has become an important part of our week. I also now have the confidence to study the Bible within my cell rather than pushing it to the back of my drawer – it has been a huge help.'

L. 'I grew up with a loving supportive family yet for some reason I was an insecure nervous child. In my early teens I tried drink and drugs – mostly "party" drugs to begin with as they made me confident enough to join in and to talk to people. They made me feel how I thought other people felt. When I was seventeen-years-old, I got into a relationship with a much older man. He was abusive in every sense of the word and I fell pregnant. We finally parted ways when the last violent encounter caused me to go into labour and my daughter was born nine weeks and five days early, at only three pounds and twelve ounces. I moved back in with my mum. I was really depressed and attempted suicide. Thankfully my mum found me and got me to hospital in time. I got myself back on track, or at least I gave the illusion I was back on track.

I moved into my own flat and I ended up taking heroin and Valium. My life was a mess. When I was twenty-one, I had my youngest daughter. This was enough to cause me to rein in the drug abuse a little, as I was on methadone, but I still took amphetamine and was always trying to fill the void inside of me. Things then got worse again. During this time, I would have people in my flat drinking and taking drugs to all hours of the night. Finally, when my girls were three and six, they were taken into foster care. I then had no reason to even try and hold it together anymore.

The next ten years is just a bit of a blur due to drink, drugs and abusive relationships as well as the chaos. I felt so empty, so lost. It was so bad that I cut my wrists and would burn my arms with cigarettes.

I think in some way I thought that I deserved the beatings that I was getting. It wasn't so bad but it was a regular enough occurrence. Some instances were worse than others. Finally, in December 2010 I was in a flat with two of us drinking and taking drugs, when a man got beaten to death, which was, in hindsight, a certainty to happen sooner or later, given how comfortable and familiar the people around me were with violence and how often it occurred.

I was remanded for murder along with the other man. All alone, isolated in a cell with no drink or drugs and the firm belief that nothing on earth could help me, I had no option but to fall on my knees and say,

"… Please God help me!"

During those ten years of carnage, I had often turned up at a mission supplying meals or an outreach bus offering a cup of tea and a chat. I had on occasions gone along to church with my mum's friend. The wonderful Christian folk I would meet at these places had something I didn't have, for they seemed to have a peace and a joy that I had never known and never thought I would know, and some of what they told me must have been held in my mind or heart somehow. That night in my prison cell was the first time I had ever truly prayed from my heart. I'd often prayed before but it was more like bargaining, saying, 'God you get me out of this, I won't do this again,' but on that night I was totally beat. I was totally willing to do things God's way. I started reading the Bible and going to church and praying on a daily basis. From that day to this day God has blessed me in so many wonderful ways. I am no longer in the clutches of addiction and I have gained many qualifications and skills. I have learnt to play the guitar and I enjoy playing in the church service and fellowship. I was allowed to speak at a conference at Edinburgh University, I attend gym five days a week and, at forty-three I am fitter and healthier than I was at twenty-one. I even got to mend some fences with my oldest daughter who was, because of my lack of ability to care for her, full of anger and resentment and who could blame her?

My daughter actually ended up in beside me in prison, although only for a short time, but it gave us a chance to spend time together and for her to see the person that I had become – although she struggled, I feel we did benefit from it. At the last Prison Fellowship group, before she got out, she said she decided to say something and I did not know what she would say! She said, "last week we read about how Christians should be more Christ-like – patient, caring, loving, kind – well that's just my mum." I was filled with emotion and still am just remembering it. It was a wonderful moment. I'm so lucky that she allows me in her life. I only pray that I can get a chance to make it up to her when I'm released. Her sister was adopted by the foster carer but maybe one day, down the line she will be in touch.

I've been inside almost eleven years and I have another four years to go, but I know that God is using me to show others his goodness. I know I have the same joy and peace that I see in the Christian people. I had to come to prison for God to set me free and in June 2015, me and my friend were baptised- a full immersion – during the fellowship meeting, with the Governor, the SPS Chaplaincy Adviser, fellow prisoners all there – and my mum and sister and nieces were able to attend. It was such a wonderful evening.'

D. has written about her life with reference to some important milestones in her journey.

D. '**The beginning** – I always had the feeling there was something more to life, something bigger than myself, bigger than all mankind. I couldn't explain what that something was but I knew that there was something waiting for me. I would find out much later. "You came into this world screaming and have never shut up since!" my mum laughed, smiling at me. "I was the first person to see you. We didn't know what to expect," my grandmother Janet adds. "It was Easter Friday and your granny always joked: 'Don't go into labour on a Friday as that's the only night me and Eddie get to go out'" – my mum pulled a silly face to mimic my gran's voice. "But you were too nosey, you couldn't wait and the doctors warned us you may not survive. I mean you were born so early, twenty-six-weeks early. It was touch and go your poor mum was only fifteen as well." Gran goes on to say: "You weighed the same as a bag of sugar, one pound eight ounces, the size of my hand" my mum's eyes cloud over as she remembers it all. So here I was, "D" which is Hebrew and means "God has judged." God was there in the beginning. As it says in Jeremiah 29:11: "For I know the plans I have for you declares the Lord plans to give you a hope and a future."

Imagination – "Abigail? Who are you talking to?" my father asks popping his head around the bedroom door. Daddy is tall with black hair and a shell suit rustles when he moves, "Can't you see her?" I say pointing to the ceiling light. This must be a game he is playing. Why can I see her sometimes? I stare at her so long the brightness of the light hurts my eyes; Abigail (my imaginary friend) is so beautiful! My dad scoops me up and holds me close, tumbling down my bed the covers billow around me as he tucks in the sheet around me. I like it when my daddy is home from work. My big cousin Chris told me that he wasn't at his work, but he was in prison, but I'm not listening to him because my daddy wouldn't tell me lies. Chris is only jealous because he doesn't have a guardian angel. Religion was never spoken about in our house. The family was divided, half Catholic, half Protestant. Being from the West of Scotland our mindset associated religion with football. I didn't understand how this fitted in with God. I mean I had never heard of Jesus popping up at a game of football!

Age five – My dad's away to work again and I can't wake up my mum. I pull a chair into the dark hallway to open the front door. It's dark outside and I walk to my nana's house because I'm hungry. 'You come and stay with us now until your mum's better', my aunt tells me. My stomach is turning over like a tumbleweed in the wind. My pulse quickens as I glance at the clock – tick-tock – the sound echoes in my head. It is nearly time. I bite my lip looking around the room. All around me people are shuffling, shoes scuffing, nervous twitches, the time seems to stand still as I glance at the clock once more. I take a deep breath and listen to the ticking impersonating my heartbeat, tick-tock, tick-tock. At last, the school bell rings. I leave my seat in excitement and shove the book I've been holding into my school rucksack. I leave the classroom and collect my coat from the peg. All around me are smiling faces, each of them happy to be going home. Not me, today I'm leaving, today my granny's picking me up and we're going to England.

England – The sound of the glass shattering makes me sit up in bed. I am fully aware, with a feeling of fear rising from my toes. My sister Molly snuggles closer to me. I pull up the covers and tuck them under her chin, as angry voices rise from the party below. We hear an argument regarding furniture then World War 3 breaks loose. I tell Molly to stay with me and she and I pray silently. I tiptoe barefooted along the landing to the top of the stairs. Panic is starting to take hold as I hold my breath, scared, as the anger pours out below. Different voices shouting, trying to be heard. Someone's trying to calm the situation down, when the front door slams. Someone attempts to make a joke, "just have another drink" a voice screams out. My stepdad is not in the mood and I hear a bang as he strikes my mum. She begins to scream as he drags her by the hair into the kitchen. I stop deadly still as I hear the second bang as he crunches her, hitting her face off a tiled floor.

Age twelve – I instantly feel better as the cap snaps and the fizzy bubbles of the cider fill my cup. Breakfast is served; the room is cold and smells of urine. I try to sleep as doors slam around me, different voices echoing down the corridor. I feel an itchy blanket as I try to get comfortable. It's another night in the cells. A few short years later a deadpan voice filled the courtroom, "you are a menace to society, a danger to yourself and others. I have no option but to sentence you to four years imprisonment. Take her down." I thought I knew it all. Full of bravado, a cocky smile and a swagger to cover up my insecurities. I felt I was hopeless, lost, alone, feeling unloved and unwanted. My daughter Molly was taken into care. My partner Kev was murdered whilst I was inside. God pulled me close and I started going to church. Eager to learn more, I began to read my Bible daily. Here I learnt of God's love for me: "For God so loved the world that he gave his only begotten son that whoever believes in him shall not perish but have eternal life." John 3:16.'

Age twenty-three – I am standing there on the tracks, the world begins to move in slow motion. I did not want to die but was so caught up in my own self-pity. So drunk I thought it would be ok. I should have walked 100 metres to walk over the bridge. "You will be fine" the Devil on my shoulder told me. Yeah, looks like it now. A train is heading straight for me. It freezes me to the spot. All I can smell is the oil and the sound of the screeching metal. I can't move, too late! I wait to start drifting, to be taken away floating to Heaven. I open my eyes. I am shaking but alive. I pull myself from under the train. I feel numb. My arms and legs are all intact, but blood is dripping down my face. 'We need you to go to hospital,' a police officer says kindly as he guides me towards the waiting ambulance. When I feel alone, I thought I had no one. I thought that no one cared – but God was there to protect me – God is faithful. "You will not be tempted beyond what you can bear, but when you are tempted, he will provide a way out so you can stand up under it" (1 Corinthians 10:13). "So how did you get them stitches in your eye?" he asked. "I was hit by a train" I reply. "Pull the other one!" I pulled out the discharge papers from my bag. "There," I say pointing to it in black and white. "You've been lucky" Robert says as he stands to go to the toilet. Robert asked to see if I would be interested in a date. "Let me think about it."'

Age twenty-five – "If you don't stop drinking, you will die!" the doctor says. "If you carry on you'll develop pancreatitis and the damage will be too far advanced. Morphine won't kill your pain." I have to go to rehab, mum's addiction worker states. I do not want the same fate.'

One year later – "I wish you could have been here to see her. She is gorgeous! I can't believe she is ours." I say. Robert and I gaze adoringly down at our newborn daughter.'

Today I am once again incarcerated but this time it is different, the difference is within me. A friend suggested I go to Prison Fellowship. When I first attended, I noticed there was a very different atmosphere. It was as if you could leave your mask behind, the mask you wore back in the hall. You could be yourself, everyone is warm and welcoming. I started going regularly and decided to be baptised. When I felt unloved and unwanted, God had carried me through the tough times and is always there to love, care for and protect me. With time my faith has grown, and I am always astonished that God is always there, ready to forgive no matter what, as long as we let him into our hearts and lives. I am slowly becoming more confident and have taken part in plays and singing in front of others. I am also doing studies with the university, even though I was recently diagnosed as having dyslexia. With God on my side, I believe I can achieve anything. The members of the Prison

Fellowship are now my extended family and mean everything to me. I cannot imagine how my time would be without their support and encouragement. Yes, I sometimes get stick from other prisoners, but if only they would open their hearts to Jesus they too could feel at ease and have the support and guidance so they are not consumed by negativity and sin.'

Chapter 4

Men's Voices

Most of the people in Scotland's prisons are men. In this chapter three of them tell their personal stories in their own words. They give an insight into the life experiences of many men in prison, the difficulties they faced in childhood, at home, in school and in their community and the choices they made – and the faith they found in prison. You will notice common themes to the life experiences the men share.

M. 'At the start of 2017, I found myself at a major crossroads in my life. I was mentally, emotionally and spiritually broken. I had been in prison for four years at that point and had one more year still to do. I had been in and out of prison since I was sixteen and I was now forty-four years old. Before prison, I spent four years in care, so it's fair to say I've spent most of my life in various institutions. I was abused while in care which, needless to say, had a major traumatic effect on my life. No longer was it only my feelings of being abandoned and unloved by my own family weighing on my young shoulders and mind, but I was now being abused by the very people being charged with taking better care of me. I established a deep-rooted hatred and anger towards authority figures.

I started using drugs at thirteen. It started with alcohol, cannabis and led on in later years to heroin. For me, heroin was a wonder drug that gave me a bit of respite from my thoughts and feelings that I just wanted to bury and forget. I became an addict. As a result of this I began stealing to fund my habit. The worse my drug-taking got, the worse my crimes became to fund it. To date, I've spent over twenty years in prison. I never cared for anyone or anything. The only thing that mattered to me was using drugs and finding ways and means of getting more drugs. I suppressed every emotion I ever had, under copious amounts of drugs. No one ever taught me how to positively regulate or control my anger.

Seventy per cent of my family were career criminals, bank robbers, pickpockets, shoplifters, burglars and drug-dealing gangsters, but to me, they were just my family. Getting taught life's morals and principles in that environment is confusing—lines are blurred to say the least.

My grandmother was a Christian and died when I was ten. This devastated me because I was really close to Grandma Annie. I loved her Bible stories when I was a kid. Two months before she died, she said to me, 'Now listen to me M and never forget what I'm about to tell you. Jesus loves you more than Grandma does, and you don't have many good role models around you. So if you ever need help, you will find it in this book'; she was holding her Bible. So all these years later at this crossroads in my life, I start to think of Grandma Annie, and I find myself asking what she would tell me to do. The answer was as clear as day, "Read your Bible".

I requested to see the Prison Chaplain and saw him the same day. I asked for a Bible and some guidance, and I was invited to go to the Prison Fellowship group. I went along with an open mind and was given a Gideon Bible with the daily reading planner. I was also given directions on how to pray. I became a regular at church and Prison Fellowship, and also attended the six-week Sycamore Tree course, which deals with victim empathy, something I had been struggling with. I was struggling with strong feelings of guilt for every victim of my crimes and all the emotional scars I left in my wake. My family was not immune to my crimes either. I was basically struggling to live with my conscience.

Prayer and daily readings became the cornerstone of my life. I was reading my Bible and for the first time understanding it: it had come to life. Needless to say, I could not stick to the daily reading plan. I would become so obsessed – before I knew it, I had read one month's selected readings in a few days. I try to read it and apply to my daily life. I've been through emotional turmoil, but in the Lord, I found serenity. As it says in Matthew 11:28: "Come unto me all you who are weary and heavy burdened and I will give you rest."

I turned my will and my life over to the Lord and became a born-again Christian on 18.11.17. Even though I'm in prison, I've never felt so free in my life. I have balance and serenity in my life, and the only thing I crave is pure spiritual nutrition. I live my life in the now. My past no longer weighs me down, and tomorrow will look after itself. My only goal is to clothe myself with compassion, kindness, humility, gentleness and patience, and over all these virtues, love. I am aware I'm a representative of Jesus. I know I fall short from time to time, but as long as the Lord is my shepherd I'll not be afraid. I pray that more prisoners will come to understand Jesus is 'standing at their door' and open it, and come to know the peace and love of the Lord Jesus for themselves.'

A. 'I have experienced the benefits and see the importance of Prison Fellowship. Firstly, in the Bible, the meaning of 'fellowship' is unity among friends. A closeness and a common partnership in society. Imagine that? Even in prison, you can have unity with others despite your conviction or lifestyle. You can be friends with a closeness that only Jesus can bring about and you can have a common partnership with anyone, not only fellow cons or staff, but also a partnership with those folks who come into prison as volunteers and yet may have none of the life experiences that you or I have had. This is insane and not the normal mindset within a jail, but it is true and I am not some happy go lucky maniac who is off his head!

I live in the North West of Scotland (Isle of Lewis to be precise.) Since I was about eleven years old I have been addicted to drink and then at fourteen, I started using drugs as well. Anything at all to get me as far away from life as possible, as with most addicts. If we are honest, we all use in order to run away from pain, hurt, fear and emotional torture given by the hands or mouths of others. After a few years, nothing can take the pain away, which makes us even more desperate and alone, using all our hurt against others and making them pay for our shortcomings. So read the above paragraph again and try to imagine having that level of deep, trusting, meaningful friendship and unity filled with peace. Insane right? Not for the Lord Jesus it isn't, and nowadays, even being able to write a sentence like that is a huge testimony to the change within my life and the part prison and Prison Fellowship has played in it.

In 2014 I was charged with attempted murder. I was given bail and during this period of bail the Lord came into my life and gave me a totally new and different perspective. I could see hope and purpose, and, for the first time ever, I actually experienced joy in my life – even through the struggles and pain and fear. Even during life on bail as an addict. In January 2015 I was sentenced to six years with a three -year extension and spent a couple of months in HMP Barlinnie, then a couple of months in HMP Glenochil before moving up to HMP Grampian for the rest of my time. So, it is obvious that my perspective comes from my experience of Prison Fellowship Scotland in HMP Grampian. This testimony is not about me but PF. I, however, had to set the context of my life in the light of the Lord and PF.

As I moved up to HMP Grampian I immediately contacted the Chaplaincy team and began to connect with Prison Fellowship – as this addicted maniac had a new life to lead and an awful lot of work to undertake within himself. Otherwise, there was no point in anything, for if I could not embrace life in the Lord among all His people, I may as well be dead. I had lived all my life desperate to die, now I actually wanted life and have a hope which I could rely on.

I attended the Tuesday night fellowship meetings, where I began to get to know the PF volunteers, who gave of their own time and love to come inside and fellowship with cons who were willing and open to change, willing to let go of their pride and willing to try and trust folks, maybe for the first time in their lives. Also having other similar minded guys from the halls there helped to relax me as many men in prison are doubtful and unsure. The main point of Prison Fellowship is freedom through faith in the Lord Jesus Christ (Gal. 5: 1), and contentment despite all our circumstances (2 Cor. 4:7-15.) This is surely enough of an appraisal of PF, because this is surely all that is needed! The beautiful truth is the light and love of the Lord and peace relying on the power of God. Everything that is trustworthy and true, everything that is just and good, everything that is peace-giving (Philippians 4: 8) – these are the reasons for PF. Actually, all of the above can be found and held onto in even the thickest darkness, no matter how bad it was, or is, or you think it will be for us. Yet the Lord Jesus, through His faithful servants, will shine a glowing light into your life. Neither life imprisonment, nor the darkest, most fearful, addiction can stop the Lord and His love from shining. The most peaceful, warm and loving "hit" you have ever had is nothing compared to the lasting love of the Lord Jesus. This is my experience!

Prison Fellowship meetings are a place for us to leave the halls behind, to focus on something bigger and more of a priority than all our problems. To share with others what we need help for. To know the effectiveness of prayer. Do you feel the gentleness and sincerity of those volunteers who want to pray for you? Can you imagine the 'Lord of Sea and Sky', who nurtures the cosmos and galaxy and other things too big for me to know? Can you imagine that same Lord wanting to pour out His generous blessings on you? Can you imagine this same Lord wanting to restore you and even listen to your prayers? Can you imagine that? Can you imagine the love that He has put into His people who serve PF, who also want all these same truths to be enjoyed in your life?

Can you imagine freedom, not from those walls and bars that are only for a time, but freedom that lasts and releases you from your fears? This next truth is enormous! But can you imagine restoration?

Yes, Prison Fellowship hold weekly meetings which are an exploration of God's Word and all Jesus said and did, offering the possibility of entering into what Jesus describes as 'life in all its fullness' (John 10: 10).

Prison Fellowship also run "Sycamore Tree" courses, which I wisely invested my time in. What is restoration? Well it is the business of God. This Restorative Justice Sycamore Tree course is 'faith based but not faith promoting'. It focuses on changing mindsets. Do you know what it is like to have a mindset impregnated with hopelessness? Restorative Justice courses break into that hopelessness by changing mindsets – if you are willing of course. For me, it was truly mind-blowing yet truly true. By running through this relatively short course, which has a powerful effect on the participants, one can try and address his/her own thought patterns. Sycamore Tree is unlike other courses – it encourages you to ask if you truly want to see an inner change of mind. The most fundamental part of the Sycamore Tree's course is associated with the Bible passage, Luke 19:1-10, when Zacchaeus came down from the tree and the Lord Jesus said to him, "Today I shall stay at your house". Whatever Jesus said, or whatever He and Zacchaeus discussed in their conversation over that meal, Zacchaeus was so challenged about his behaviour and lifestyle, he changed his attitude and behaviour, giving back to those he had cheated and showing generosity to those in need. Changed inside out and for good! This is the primary purpose of Sycamore Tree: that you will address your offending behaviour and show this by your actions and also that you may want to join the PF conversational group to explore how God can change you from the inside. This is the power of Jesus' Good News which saves us from our past and our wrong attitudes and calls us to serve Him.

Prison Fellowship was my only constant in a changing environment. It is a genuine pathway toward rehabilitation. Jesus' Good News offers the freedom from all our pasts and Prison Fellowship, as part of Chaplaincy, can be a huge part in helping us understand the glory and grace of Christ. The Lord Jesus changes lives and Prison Fellowship, by God's goodness and grace, is a vehicle for that to happen. Thank God for all those who gladly and willingly give of their own time to serve others, and they do not even do these things by their own merit but Christ who lives within them.

No matter what name the course holds or who you fellowship with or who sits with you and prays for you, no matter what prison you are in or where in your journey you are, only one thing is unchanging and that is the love of God. We know or will come to know that God works all things together for good to those who love Him (Rom. 8:28.) I thank God for Prison Fellowship and its army of volunteers. In my view, their regular and committed service of men and women in prison is a physical demonstration of God's love and care. The volunteers, who work for PF, whether I know them or not, are in my heart and prayers for the very special work they do. Prison Fellowship groups in prison are a much-needed safe place inside an environment of apparent hopelessness.'

A. 'HMP Glenochil is where I spent my nearly three year sentence. Me and the others attending Prison Fellowship were invariably laughed at each Tuesday night as we went to the chapel. There were usually around twenty of us per evening varying in nationalities, religions, and core beliefs. There are no barriers to attending fellowship; we had Christians, Catholics, Muslims and Hindus as well as non-believers attending. It was great – those of different faiths all respecting each other. I found it really interesting to learn about faiths that I had not even asked about. The group was held during rec time, so we were all there because we wanted to be – no-one was there ticking boxes or escaping work parties. This made it work well.

Each week we would do different things at the group but we would always start off the session with a time of praise, usually three hymns, followed by a time of prayer. Some weeks we would have quiz competitions, other times Bible studies, watching films or doing the Alpha courses and we always had time to generally chat and chew things over. The evening always ended with coffee, then a closing prayer. The way it was organised and facilitated made you feel worth something and respected. The leaders never failed to turn up for the weekly sessions, irrespective of how deep the snow was outside. They truly reflected Jesus in the way they always treated the inmates with respect, never ever judging any one of us and without fail, treated every inmate as an individual person.

During my sentence, I completed the Restorative Justice course Prison Fellowship run called the 'Sycamore Tree Course'. Our Course was held on Tuesday mornings. This activity was limited to about six prisoners in order to prevent people using the group to miss work commitments! Completing the course was one of the most catalytic events of my imprisonment. I was nine months into my sentence when I embarked on it and it marked the onset of me making a journey that is still in progress. The course is based on the story of the wee man

Zacchaeus climbing the Sycamore Tree and meeting with Jesus in a life-changing way. For me, it was not merely a story, but a challenging and hopeful reality, that is still achievable for me. The most impacting part for me was the demonstration of the ripple effect and when out of the blue an orange is thrown into a basin of water and we see the mess it makes and start to unpack the realities of the effects our crimes have had. For me, this brought a sudden realisation that no matter how far I was from the epicentre of the damage I had created when I committed my offence, I was not immune to the consequences of the damage or the hurt I had caused. As I processed what we were being presented, each week came the recognition and awareness that life was not all about me, in fact, it was the complete opposite. For me, that was a stark revelation. Without trying to be too dramatic, it changed my life around in spectacular fashion. The course gave me the opportunity and the support to start to make life changes that will hopefully ripple in a positive way.

Coming out of prison was not the end of my journey. The road I am travelling on has no end. It is not always a smooth motorway often narrowing. At times the days are darker than they should be but the road I started in HMP Glenochil, under the leadership of the Prison Fellowship, is a lot more than manageable now.

It's strange to say but today I am in a far better place than I have ever been in my life. Yes, I know there have been tough consequences to pay, but the journey I started has enabled me to seek the right help, have the right people in my life, as well as being part of a church family. Today I have an accountability partner who is part of the church family and also who delivers Prison Fellowship within Grampian. Despite being on my own, I have been blessed; I have become enriched by God's presence.'

Chapter 5

Volunteer Voices

If you were to read only the last two chapters you might imagine that Prison Fellowship Scotland volunteers are super-human, saintly creatures! In fact, they are ordinary folk from a variety of Christian backgrounds, traditions and denominations. They are the human face of PFS and the weekly contact with men and women in prison throughout Scotland. They are literally the heart of our work. Here they will tell you their own stories.

You have already heard about Our Victim Awareness / Restorative Justice Course, Sycamore Tree Course. Edith has been part of the team at HMP Low Moss since the new prison opened and gives more detail of its content.

Edith

Act Towards

' As I approached retirement, I began to think of how I could now use my training and experience in the Christian Voluntary Sector. I began my career as a secondary school teacher in a deprived area. Soon I realised that when a young person's home environment is challenging, it impacts on their school life; as such, students were not in a state, emotionally, to allow me to teach them the intricacies of chemistry and biology. This led me to the pastoral side of teaching which concentrates on caring for every aspect of pupils' welfare to enable them to reach their potential.

After a break to focus on my family and working as a partner in the family business, I returned to my first love – teaching. This time

I worked with pupils who found, for many and complex reasons, that life in mainstream education was not the right option for them. Some were exhibiting confrontational behaviour and making some poor life choices. Although challenging, this was a rewarding and often emotional experience, but I was aware of God's strength, giving me love and compassion for them, many of whom had experienced little love and security in their lives. As the time in my role as a teacher was coming to an end because retirement approached, I knew that I would miss not only the challenges which teaching offered, but also the social interaction. I therefore asked God to show me how He wanted me to continue to use my qualifications and experience. The answer came one evening at a dinner where the speaker was Billy Paul of Prison Fellowship. He spoke about the work of Prison Fellowship and especially the Sycamore Tree Course which was being rolled out into Scottish Prisons.

The course is designed to bring offenders to a meaningful realisation of the spectrum of victims of their crime and the impact of their crime on these individuals. Volunteers were needed to deliver the course, which seemed to involve the very teaching and pastoral care skills I had developed over the course of my career. The words from Matthew 25: 36 – 'I was in prison and you visited me' – kept going through my head and it was as if God was speaking directly to me that evening. Was I being called to assist with this work? Did my experience of working with disadvantaged young people and my desire to help others help qualify me? At the end of the evening I spoke with Billy and was handed an application form there and then. After being interviewed and accepted, I was trained (a) by Prison Fellowship in their aims and values, as well as in-depth training on how to deliver Sycamore, and (b) by the Scottish Prison Service (which included learning a whole new prison vocabulary and rules for volunteers). Only then was I ready to become part of the group of volunteers in Low Moss delivering The Sycamore Tree Course.

The Sycamore Tree Course introduces participating prisoners to Restorative Justice and helps to raise their awareness of the wider impact of their crime using the story of Zacchaeus the tax collector (Luke 19), who was taking excess taxes from his own people but, after his meeting with Jesus, showed remorse and turned his life around. Restorative Justice considers the needs and feelings of the victims of crime in stark contrast to traditional Retributive Justice, which only considers the punishment of the offender. Sycamore leads prisoners to face the fact that there are many and diverse victims of their crime – not only the direct victim(s) but also the prisoners' immediate family, their community, etc., all of whom are impacted by the crime and/or subsequent imprisonment of the prisoner. The course is delivered using a combination of integrated short DVDs, discussion groups, and direct teaching. It takes place in an open and non-threatening environment, and always incorporates the all-important tea and chocolate biscuits! Over six sessions, the leaders and participants build up relationships, which are strengthened during the tea breaks when the men (in the case of Low Moss) enjoy the opportunity to relax and chat socially amongst themselves and with the team – often they open up about their past history, secure in the knowledge that the course leaders are not there to judge but rather to support them and value them as people who can make a positive contribution to society.

At Low Moss, the course takes place in the Chaplaincy Centre and we are extremely fortunate to have a great group of chaplains who are not only both accommodating and supportive of the course, but who also often actively take part in the discussions. At the end of the course, the participants are encouraged to talk to the chaplains about signing up to attend some of the other varied and helpful courses the Chaplaincy Centre has on offer.

The Sycamore Tree course weekly topics include:

- What is Restorative Justice? – This looks at what 'restore' means and how it relates to restoring relationships within a family and/or community and the effort and commitment this takes.

- Prisoners Taking Responsibility for their crime and the consequences of that crime instead of blaming others and making excuses.

- Saying Sorry and Acting Sorry – actions speak louder than words. Zacchaeus showed that he was sorry by giving half of his wealth to the poor and paying back four times the amount he had stolen.

- Reconciliation – giving and receiving forgiveness.
- Taking the Next Step.

Towards the end of the course, the participants are challenged to "ACT towards a new way of THINKING, not THINK their way towards a new way of ACTING." This would seem to contradict traditional instructions – e.g. think before you speak, look before you leap – but let's consider it from another angle. How many people, when they intend to give up smoking, say, "I'll stop after I've finished this packet" or "I'll stop on 1ˢᵗ January and that will be my New Year's resolution"? Are they successful? – Not very *often!* The only way to stop smoking is to stop thinking about it and start acting by never lighting up another cigarette. How can this philosophy be applied by the offenders? By thinking about how their actions have affected their victims, offenders can use their time in prison to consider what they will do when they leave. If they do not start changing their way of acting towards others and put preparations in place before they leave, they can easily fall back into their old way of life and reoffending quickly follows.

So, what can the offenders do in prison to turn their lives around and prepare for the future? Something as simple as apologising to a partner or family for the impact that their stay in prison has had on the partner/family can be a powerful and thereafter motivating start. For example, on one occasion, following the part of the course where giving and receiving forgiveness had been discussed, a participant apologised to his partner for her stress, which had been caused by his actions and subsequent prison sentence. He asked for her forgiveness and was amazed when she told him that she had already forgiven him. We were delighted when, the following week, he reported back to us, showing genuine and very raw emotion, and admitted that he had never apologised to anyone before. Another young man, when chatting over tea and biscuits, confided that he had cut off contact with his mother and grandmother. We reflected with him on this and I was delighted to hear the next week that it had resulted in him phoning them to apologise and tearful reconciliations had taken place. Other examples of positive starts include offenders starting to ask friends and family how they were coping outside the prison (instead of the prisoners focussing on how they, personally, were "suffering" by being in prison), offenders signing up for a drug or alcohol rehabilitation course immediately upon release, etc. Not only do these actions directly help the offender but they also demonstrate to others that they genuinely intend to stop their offending and/or related behaviour.

Already established in England as part of the criminal justice system, the full programme of Restorative Justice affords an offender the chance to apologise to his/her victim(s) and to hear from the victim(s) the impact that the crime has had on them. This has had a positive effect on the reoffending rate. Unfortunately, at present in Scotland, there is no system in place whereby an offender can, after a period of preparation of both the victim and offender, meet with his/her victim for the purpose of taking this restorative step. After taking part in the Sycamore Tree Course, many of our participants have expressed frustration that the opportunity is not available in Scotland to have a facilitated meeting with their direct victim. This is a powerful reflection on the impact the course has on its participants. I am always encouraged to see that the Sycamore Tree Course is continually being revised and updated; there are plans to introduce follow-up courses which would further enhance and reinforce the restorative justice message and this can only be a positive step, but it is important that we continue, in Scotland, to push for more comprehensive Restorative Justice to allow the good work in prisons to be fully spread into the community.

What have the Sycamore Tree course and the offenders themselves taught me personally about Acting towards a new way of Thinking? Male offenders, like the men we work with, are all some mother's son or someone's husband or father. As such, we – the community at large – must treat them as we would want our own son/husband/father to be treated. Prisoners have made some bad life choices – but haven't we all made mistakes? Many inmates never imagined that they would ever find themselves in that position and one poor decision, perhaps under the influence of drink and/or drugs, should not commit them, after serving their sentence, to a future with no prospects. We must always remember that offenders are loved by Jesus – He weeps for them all. I have wept for them too. Offenders are one prayer away from the saving grace of God – we all have to repent of our sins. We must pray for the prisoners to come to know His loving forgiveness and prisoners, like all of us, need to forgive themselves for past mistakes and know that only Jesus' love is unconditional.

I feel honoured and privileged to have been given the chance, in a very small way and with God's help, to guide offenders towards a better, non-offending future. To a much greater extent, the experiences of the participants of the course who have changed their ways of thinking provide them with so much to offer the community in many and diverse ways. They have the credibility to visit schools and talk to young people who can relate to them and who may be heading for a life of crime. This relationship gives them the opportunity to warn them of the ultimate risks of their poor lifestyle choices and thus hopefully steer others in a more positive direction. Similarly, their own experiences of addiction enable them to relate to addicts when volunteering in rehab centres, etc. – again, affording them the opportunity to give back to society. It is especially uplifting to hear of ex-offenders who now have a close relationship with God and are working as pastors or other Christian leaders. I pray for the work of Prison Fellowship Scotland, especially that Sycamore Tree will continue to develop and flourish in our prisons and that many lives will be touched by God through the work and commitment of everyone involved.'

Derek

Derek was a serving prison officer and has been involved in PFS from its very beginnings. Even while serving as a prison officer, Derek was a weekly volunteer with PFS, working beyond hours to make himself available for the groups.

'I have been retired from the Scottish Prison Service for over twenty years, joining the service in November 1966. My first posting was Castle Huntly on the main Dundee Perth Road. I retired from

Greenock prison on the 5th of May 1998. In between these years, I was transferred to Greenock then to Cornton Vale and then some years later back to Greenock, where I still live. I am originally from Aberdeen where I lived till I was almost twenty-three-years-old.

When I started, Castle Huntly was an open borstal for lads aged sixteen to twenty-one. The lads were sentenced to a maximum period of three years to undergo "borstal training". It was considered quite revolutionary at the time. The thinking behind the sentence was that the trainees could determine how long they spend in custody. After each month they were assessed as to their progress, and if consistent progress was seen to be made, they could be released within six to nine months. Some lads served the full three years, but the vast majority were released before the three years were up.

It was a staff (who were not in uniform) intensive system – each officer was assigned a group of around a dozen lads to look after and report on. You met with the lads individually on a weekly and monthly basis. Each lad was given a written report, which was given to him to read and respond to. You could join them at the visits and chat with their families; it was a bit like Parents Night at school. There was real intention to have the families involved in the sentence. You got to know the lads very well and addressed them by their first names. Because it was an open setting, there were lads, surprisingly few I have to say, who were sent back to Polmont to continue their training there. Polmont, near Falkirk, was the main Borstal; it was where every lad sentenced to Borstal training went for assessment before being transferred to Castle Huntly or to another Borstal near Forfar called Noranside.

Borstal training came to an end probably around the early to mid-1980s when the young offenders sentence was introduced – the prisoner was given two liberation dates known as the "earliest date of liberation" (EDL) and the "latest date of liberation" (LDL). The thinking behind the sentence was that the prisoner would be released at the earlier date should he behave himself, and at a later date if not. The prisoner could lose remission because his behaviour did not come up to a set standard; the Governor of the prison had the authority to take remission from a prisoner at the orderly room. The prisoner could request to be given back lost remission if his behaviour improved.

There was a Statutory Body set up by the government called the "Visiting Committee", which a prisoner could appeal to if he thought the punishment was unfair. The governor could also request the visiting committee to sit in judgement on a prisoner because they had the authority to take more remission than the governor. That system has now been overtaken by the current system.

Male officers working with women doing personal training, was an experiment that began around 1971. I was transferred to the borstal section in Greenock prison from Castle Huntly in 1972 as part of this new experiment. The experiment was successful and continues to this day with female staff working alongside male prisoners. For me working with women was quite a challenge. Boys being in prison seemed somehow quite normal to me. Girls in prison for me, at least, was far from normal. This involved a huge learning curve. I had become used to having lads dressed in Battledress uniform with tackety boots on out on the parade square doing matching manoeuvres, taking them out in the country, picking potatoes ("tatties"), raspberries or strawberries, cutting down trees and sawing branches into logs, fairly physical, manly stuff. In Greenock, the lassies wore floral dresses, makeup and worked at sewing machines. The staff members were all female. It took me a little while to get used to it all. Around that time Cornton Vale prison in Bridge of Allan, a new women's prison, was near completion and once it was open for business I was transferred there. Another change was in store for me – cells were done away with and the women had rooms, cell keys became almost obsolete and electronic locking and unlocking was in use. Women could get out of the rooms at night to use toilet facilities – all very new to me.

It was whilst at Cornton Vale that a new venture opened up for me. The Governor, Lady Martha Bruce, was keen for staff to become more involved in creating activities for the girls. I was given permission to begin a Bible class; I was also given permission to invite folks from local Churches to form a group to join me in this new activity. We held the class in the beautiful purpose-built Chapel. As things do, it began slowly, but within a fairly short period of time around thirty women were attending the class. I was contacted by a Mrs Louise Purvis and asked if I would meet with her and other Christians to discuss the possibility of forming a group recently founded in England called Prison Christian Fellowship. Within a very short time Prison Fellowship Scotland was formed, with its first-ever group starting in Barlinnie. The group that I was leading in Cornton Vale was now also under the banner of Prison Fellowship Scotland. The name was quickly shortened to PF and quickly took hold. PF has now been running for forty years and has groups in thirteen of the fifteen Scottish Prisons.

In the 1980s serious trouble broke out, first of all in Peterhead prison and then spreading to other major prisons. It became national news night after night. Eventually the Army was called in and in a fairly short time, the prisoners were brought back under control but not before millions of pounds worth of damage was done. Many staff and prisoners were seriously hurt; something had to be done with the ringleaders who were spread around the prison estate. Greenock prison, now empty of prisoners, was being refurbished to go up to category A security level. The intention was it would hold many of the troublemakers. I was asked if I would consider transferring to Greenock and after discussing the matter with my wife Marion, we, along with our three children, moved to Greenock. This would be the first time I would be working with long-term adult male prisoners. I would also now need to wear a uniform.

Another first for me, took place at Greenock. The principal officer said to me, 'Mr Watt we have a problem with you. We don't know what division to put you in. We believe you are a Christian but we don't know whether you are a Catholic or Protestant Christian.' I said to him, as far as I was concerned I was a Christian, and I would be happy to work on either division.

The Deputy Governor at Greenock was also a Christian and it was he who had contacted me regarding a transfer to Greenock and asked me to start a Prison Fellowship group. The prison quickly filled up with a number of very notorious and dangerous prisoners. At our first PF group, around a dozen came. It became clear they had not come for Bible study but to discuss among themselves how they were going to run the prison – yes you have read correctly! It took time for us to get control of things but eventually, we got their attention and explained to them about PF and what we hoped to do at Greenock. Before the evening finished, we all stood in a circle with our arms around each other's shoulders and said the Lord's Prayer together – a night I will never forget and a night that began for me the most enjoyable three years of my time in the prison service.

Forty years have passed, I am now retired but PF continues to flourish. My health is good, and I am able to do PF volunteer work in Barlinnie and Greenock. We have a couple of excellent teams of volunteers with at least five of the Greenock volunteers having been with us for over thirty years and still going strong. We have three groups per week at Barlinnie and four groups at Greenock. We have witnessed many lives changed for the glory of the Lord.'

Kathryn

'I've been a volunteer for five years and during that time I also worked for six months as Volunteer Co-ordinator for PFS. I have been challenged, humbled and encouraged by the woman in the Prison Fellowship group. As a result, my own faith has been reshaped and re-invigorated to become a faith to be lived, rather than one that remains on a page. During a series of structured conversations I held with various women, a common theme came up again and again – '... Being part of the group has helped me feel human again'. The importance of belonging to the group mattered hugely and created a space for people to meet as equals, both in need of God's mercy and in need of connection with other human beings. Watching these women wrestle with issues such as low self-esteem, shame, guilt and fear in an environment that does not always feel safe for them, challenged me: how on earth would I respond in similar circumstances. Just like me, they are seeking acceptance, peace and a sense of security.'

Margaret

' A friend invited me to join a small group of prison visitors about ten years ago. At first, I was apprehensive as I had never been in contact with anyone in prison prior to this. Like many others, I thought that the people in prison were different from me and that I would not know how to communicate with them.

I was so wrong. God gave me a real concern for those in prison and after a few years of doing this visiting, I applied to become part of Prison Fellowship. It was becoming very clear to me that those in prison needed a saviour as much as I had, and I wanted to be a part of the group who shared our faith with them.

Since joining Prison Fellowship Scotland seven years ago I have been truly blessed by the ministry. I have watched girls coming to a Fellowship meeting for the first time and hardly speaking and, as the weeks go on, the same girl is asking for her favourite hymn or asking questions about what we have been reading in Scripture.

There is real happiness when one of the women, who has come to know the Lord, is being released, but there is also a sadness knowing that often they are on their own again without the support they need, and missing the support of the Fellowship group. I never imagined when I started visiting prisoners ten years ago that I could say that I love them, but today I can honestly say that. I would love to continue this work as long as I am able and would encourage anyone who has an interest to get involved. It is so rewarding.'

Ruth

'Journeying to Perth woolly-headed in the aftermath of a migraine, I was not anticipating a day of any special significance, however God had other ideas. We arrived early to a welcome cuppa and I found my head clearing rather more quickly than usual. I was warmly welcomed by many different individuals who gathered me into their conversations about working alongside chaplains and with prisoners. It was the sense of Christian family, with no distinctions between denominations, ex-offenders, or Prison Fellowship volunteers, that grabbed my attention and compelled me to register my interest before the end of the Annual Gathering in spring 2017.

With the application process underway, it was reassuring to have regular conversations with long-standing volunteers, who kindly and patiently responded to my questions about the work of Prison Fellowship Scotland and my potential suitability. Formal training sessions were particularly helpful in highlighting the responsibilities and challenges associated with volunteering within a secure setting, as well as sharing the positive outcomes. Hearing first-hand accounts of transformed lives was so inspiring to me as a newcomer, but even more encouraging was the notion of 'the ministry of turning up', which I felt was within my capabilities.

The invitation for an initial prison visit came in the autumn and it was with considerable apprehension that I made my way to the meeting point. Simple tasks like placing my personal belongings in a locker and finding my way through security to use the public toilet that morning seemed unduly arduous, but the warmth and encouragement of the other team members put me totally at my ease, and we were soon guided through to the Chaplaincy area. The welcome I received from the prisoners was humbling, as they were at pains to make sure I felt comfortable, even offering me the best biscuits!

The opportunity to volunteer with PFS came at a time when I was feeling particularly concerned about the plight of vulnerable and isolated people in our community. I really enjoy listening to the members of the group, who are keen to chat about their life inside the prison and aspirations for the future, as well as mentioning particular problems they are facing. There have been disappointments, for example losing contact with one person, who had seemed determined to take up offers of practical help following release. However, it is a joy to spend time with the members of the group and experience their honesty in discussions about the Bible. My love for God's word has grown considerably due to the inspirational teaching I receive from the other team members during the weekly sessions, and I'm continually being challenged about my own Christian journey.'

Billy

'I did not get involved enthusiastically with PFS. I was asked by a prison officer, Derek Watt, if I would be interested in joining the recently formed Prison Fellowship Scotland group in the, newly opened, long-term prison, HMP Greenock – I remembered the words of Matthew 25 especially, "I was in prison and you visited me!" I had no choice; I could not say 'No'!

I have been a volunteer now with Prison Fellowship Scotland for forty years. I have learned a lot and enjoyed it immensely. I have met, and continue to meet, thousands of interesting people – men and women serving sentences, prison officers and volunteers. It has been inspiring to see men and women's lives, and life opportunities, changed as they decide to follow Jesus.

That first group I met with was about twenty men, many of whom had been involved in serious and violent crime. And yet at the end of each group, remarkably, volunteers, including two serving prison officers, and the men serving their sentences, held hands and prayed the Lord's Prayer together!

It was remarkable how some of those men were affected by coming to faith. I recall one man who almost shuffled into the room, head bowed and very quiet. He started to walk differently as he began to understand forgiveness. Another man, muscular, shaven head, known as a "heavy", told us he was visited, in his cell, by another prisoner who intended to assault him. He knocked his assailant to the floor but – could not kick the man he had knocked to the floor, because of the change he was experiencing in his life. Yet another small man with a violent reputation prayed – "I don't know what's happening to me but it is f...in brilliant!"

The Governor at the time, Dr Andrew Coyle, attributed the fact that the atmosphere in the prison was calm and there had been no riots (as there were in other prisons at the time) to the influence of the faith community, particularly including the men attending PF.

The Greenock group has seen all sorts of changes and currently also works with women. Again, we are privileged to help people understand and explore faith in Jesus, some of whom will also tell their own stories in this book. One outstanding moment, was the evening at a PF group when the Chaplain helped respond to a request from two of the women for baptism. The best part of that story is that those two women continue to be a positive influence in the PF group and are supportive to other women in the hall. They are able to speak honestly and clearly about their faith and its effect on their life, attitudes and behaviour. They are inspirational!

There are so many stories of men and women building a new future based on a new faith or a re-igniting of faith, in PF groups throughout Scotland, as you will hear in other chapters of this book.

Music plays a significant part in a number of our groups. As a result of one of the PF International visits in 2007, when PF Scotland was celebrating their twenty-fifth year of service, I was invited to sing at the PF International Convocation in Toronto and again, remarkably, in 2011. On the first occasion when I sang, someone at PFI googled Billy Paul and advertised me as a 'Grammy Award soul singer'! I had to disappoint everyone – I was not the Afro- American, soul singer – and that nothing was going on between 'Me and Mrs Jones'!

These were fascinating and enjoyable occasions, sharing fellowship with PF workers, volunteers and supporters from around the world, across a wide variety of denominational backgrounds. What a strong sense of purpose and of family!'

Luke

'I felt God call me into working with men and women in prison back in 2015 and so I began looking at ministries that I could connect with to make this happen. At the same time, a young guy came to work with me in my newly set up removals business, who told me that he'd been released from prison previously and was looking to start afresh. He also told me about a Christian group that he had been attending while in prison that had encouraged him and prayed for him and although he couldn't remember the name of this group, I can only imagine that it was Prison Fellowship! He'd also had a strong spiritual encounter with God upon his release that made him realise he needed change, so when I shared Jesus' Good News with him, he was ready to be a follower of Jesus and start coming to church. This incident convinced me that I should get involved in reaching out to more guys, in and out of jail.

After a lengthy wait, the door finally opened for me to become part of the Prison Fellowship group at HMP Glenochil in early 2018. I spent the first few months under the tutelage of Terry Patterson, who was at that point the Director of PF and it was great to see the men engage in the Bible teaching presented. Shortly after this, I found myself helping to lead the group directly and as someone used to leading Bible studies, I relished the chance to encourage the men to explore faith in Jesus and connect with God at a deeper level. I took the new role seriously and prepared for each Thursday with prayer and fasting. Each Thursday I could feel the struggle to get, what was going to be shared later that evening, right, but it was always worth it!

It was wonderful to see God at work in the lives of the men in the group as the year went on. Men were coming to the group that had not had any previous experience of God or church and were becoming aware of Him in their own and new ways. They expressed the appreciation and benefit of prayer.

We are privileged to be able to pray for the men and have them report that they also were praying for us. One man came for the first time and wasn't feeling well but we prayed for him, and at the end of the evening reported feeling much better. This made him want to come back the following Thursday. After coming along regularly to the group he subsequently decided to follow Jesus, even visiting a local church upon his release. He wasn't the only inmate to begin a journey of faith. A number of guys have come to us and asked about joining that journey of faith since going in. We often see a real change in the men's behaviour, when they allow God to take control of their lives that were broken and out of control, find direction, purpose and renewed motivation.

In my short time with PF, I've come to realise that some of the men will come and go and will be in and out of prison. It is important that, while challenging their wrong choices, we always treat them with respect and courtesy. Meeting some of the guys and hearing their stories makes you realise that what you are doing and sharing with them is just one small part of their life's journey of which many others contribute. Integral to the success of the groups is the ongoing work and influence of the Chaplain. Many of the men that come along have been involved with, encouraged and taught by HMP Glenochil's Chaplain, Graham Bell, who oversees all the work of the faith communities within the prison and has the pastoral care for the men, providing opportunities for men to express their faith. He is there for the men all week and we are a part of his provision for their care and exploration of faith. The other volunteers themselves are the lifeblood that keeps the group operating and bring hope and encouragement to men when they are often at their lowest and most vulnerable. It has been a real privilege and honour, working alongside Billy, Tom, Alistair, Ally, Paul and the others.

Working with the men in prison is always rewarding and worthwhile. You can go to the group tired after a long day and come home energised having seen how the guys respond and the interest they show and the contributions they make about their own journeys of faith; and hear how an area of their life has improved after praying about it. I can think of one man in particular who has responded in a really positive way. There are not many guys that are so enthusiastic to learn about God, in or out of prison, and his heartfelt prayers have been an inspiration to the other men and the volunteers alike. His interest has seen others want to know more and begin on their own faith journey.

One of the verses that motivated me to reach out to those 'inside' was Matthew 25:34-36: "Then the King will say to those on his right, "Come, you who are blessed by my Father; take your inheritance, the kingdom prepared for you since the creation of the world. For I was hungry and you gave me something to eat, I was thirsty and you gave me something to drink, I was a stranger and you invited me in, I needed clothes and you clothed me, I was sick and you looked after me, I was in prison and you came to visit me."

Giving up a couple of hours a week or every other week is a small investment in 'Your Kingdom come, Your will be done on Earth as it is in Heaven.' It's great to hear the stories of men that have reformed their character while in jail and are now serving God outside, or that have become advocates for change in some capacity. But even if we don't see the effects of our prayers, words, time and friendship with the men behind bars, we know that none of it is wasted. God's love has been shown to us and He chooses to show it through us and His love changes things and people.'

Marc

'I was first introduced to working in prison when I was invited into HMYOI Polmont by a prison officer back in 2011. I had recently become a Christian and was sharing my faith by performing rap music in and around Glasgow. A prison officer had heard my music and asked if I would come into Polmont and share my experience and perform for the inmates. This invitation kicked off a journey into prison volunteering that would shape my character and God's direction in my life.

I was invited to join Prison Fellowship Scotland in 2015 and joined the Team at HMP Addiewell. It is an incredible privilege to sit and have fellowship with the men in Addiewell.

> *... but those who hope in the LORD will renew their strength. They will soar on wings like eagles; they will run and not grow weary, they will walk and not be faint.*
> ISAIAH 40:31

There is no greater pleasure in life than seeing someone being filled with hope. Some of these men are so broken and hurt, that they have lost all hope. "Doing time" gives you time, never-ending time it would seem, to think about life, how it's turned out, your actions and your future. For most men in prison, the future seems bleak. Even if they do a short sentence, they feel forever marred with the 'criminal' label. Along with that comes the guilt and shame. But Jesus comes to offer them hope. Hope – based on forgiveness of sin (Luke 24:46-47). Hope – based on being a new creation (2 Cor. 5:17), through Jesus Christ.

Being a volunteer at Prison Fellowship is one of the greatest blessings in my life. To walk alongside the men, to talk, laugh, and cry together is such an incredible journey. In a strange paradox, spending time with them brings me hope, it encourages me, and after each fellowship night I come away feeling closer to Jesus than when I first went in. I hope to continue to serve Prison Fellowship for as long as my heart beats.'

CHAPTER 6

Sycamore Tree

Victim Awareness / Restorative Justice Course

You've heard about the course from Prison Fellowship volunteers' perspective. Now listen to the voices of participants and a governor. It has proved to be a very useful tool in helping men and women address their offending behaviour as some of our volunteers have explained and some of the men in Chapter four have commented. The first paragraphs are from retired Governor, Dan Gunn of HMP Glenochil indicating his view of the ST course. The remainder are quotes from course participants.

Dan Gunn

'..., I would like to draw your attention to the Sycamore Tree Programme. Terry Paterson, part of Prison Fellowship, has delivered two courses here, supported by our chaplain, Rev. Graham Bell. I have presented the certificates on both occasions and had the opportunity to listen to the prisoners' testimony, to use a religious term. I wish to emphasise how impressive and indeed humbling I found the experience of listening to the feedback. The last course attracted fifteen and all completed the course. This is a completion rate and group size not replicated anywhere in our Accredited Programmes. It should also be borne in mind ... there is no external incentive for the prisoners to attend .... I think it is incumbent on my part to share my very positive and uplifting experience and to encourage you to consider what you can do to spread this specific example of "good news".'

Participants' voices

- 'I think more about the impact my actions have had and caused others. It causes me to think more in-depth of the effect my actions will impact on others. I am not as blinded to my actions as before.'

- 'The course has made me think of how I live and the way I would like to live. I also have a better understanding of the things I have done and the people I have hurt ...'

- 'It made me think of everyone it affects when I commit a crime ...'

- 'I got a lot out of Sycamore Tree. It opened my eyes to the ripple effect that crime has. The effect on everyone, no matter how big or small.'

- 'The course has made me think about how much hurt is caused and the damage that is done when you commit a crime and the full extent of your actions ... This course has made me take a good look at my life and now hopefully I have the tools to go out and make a decent life for myself and my daughter. I know there is little chance of me reoffending when I am released. I have learned so much on this course and hope to pass on what I have learned to others in the future. Thanks for everything.'

- 'It made me realise the Big Picture i.e. that my actions have long-lasting and sometimes drastic consequences. It's been a year since I committed my crime and people are still feeling and will continue to feel the problems I have made. Some people's thoughts and feelings I will never be able to fix, but I'll still try, given the opportunity. My family still feels the problems – they are 100 per cent behind me and it helps me realise that I have fixed some of the problems I have made, and I need to be out of prison and properly fix everything and gain some people's trust back.'

- 'The course has made an impact on helping me see things in perspective and from the victim's point of view.'

- 'The course has made me see that my family are victims as well in my crime. In the future, I will think before I act and not act before I think. I will also try to make my son think before he acts because I don't want to see him in prison.'

- 'Sycamore has let me see the number of people that have been affected by my actions and crimes that I have committed and that there is always something I can do, no matter how big or small, to say sorry and mean it.'

- 'With me understanding more and more about retributive justice and restorative justice makes me want to have a normal life, crime-free. If I do that it will save me having victims as I won't be committing crime.'

- '… I am eager to give back to those I hurt and offended against.'

- 'Made me think about the harm and effects on victims and their families and on my family and friends. Made me realise it is going to take a long time to restore their trust in me and it will take time and a load of effort. It's made me realise it's not only me and my victim but <u>victims</u>.'

- 'I have thought more about the victims of my offences, more about how it doesn't only affect me and my direct victim but more of the ripple effect on the community … I am determined that when I get out I'll be 100 per cent focused on getting back to work and providing for my family financially and emotionally.'

CHAPTER 7

Angel Tree

Children are often the forgotten victims of crime. They need our interest and care. It is also true that one of the most significant factors in preventing reoffending is the maintenance of close family ties, so anything that helps cement those relationships is particularly important for the child, for the parent(s) and our communities. So, the Adventure Holidays for the children of parents or carers in prison, and the provision of gifts for parents in prison to give to their children at Christmas, are an important means of helping strengthen these bonds.

Summer Camps

In the introduction, there are quotes about the adventure holidays we provide in collaboration with SU Scotland and Circle Scotland's, families affected by imprisonment (FABI), workers. The feedback we have had from this project is consistently positive from Circle workers, parents and especially the more than two hundred children who have been able to attend.

The parent and child, together, can choose the type and venue for their holiday from the SU brochure. This involves the parents in the shared process of looking through the brochure, helping choose the particular holiday and join in the fun of anticipation and planning for the break. It is a positive experience for both parent(s) and child. And when they return from their adventures, there is the joy of sharing together in the reports of how it was, what they did, who they met, friends they made etc. It is an experience that helps build the bonds between parent and child.

It also has the huge added bonus that, apart from the necessary communication between SU and Circle workers, unlike school and home life, no one knows about the child's parent being in prison so they can just be one of the group, have fun and make friends at face value. The best way for us to measure the impact of this project is to listen to the remarkably positive feedback from the parents, the Circle FABI workers and the young people themselves.

Here are some of their voices:

Circle Workers

- 'All three kids loved it and thought the staff were great – Bill was mentioned quite a lot – it's always good for them to have a positive male role model so thank you, Bill!'

- 'Planning this holiday was the most enthusiastic I've seen S. S had no reservations about going and being away from her family. The only issue S. had was, could she take her phone.'

- 'I remember picking up S and her chatting away enthusiastically about all the activities that she had been doing and friends that she had made. S. had also exchanged contact numbers with a couple of her new friends who lived near her. S. spoke with confidence and I noticed that she sounded more polite. This was distinctive as S. has a slight speech impediment and often talks quickly which I sometimes find it a bit difficult to catch what she is saying. I didn't have any problems.' 'S. has since been in contact with her new friends she met on holiday and the school have reported that they have noticed a big difference in her confidence.'

- 'All the children had an amazing experience, several of these children said how difficult it was at the beginning but once settled, loved it. Some want to go back next year. One of the families that I will no longer be working with next year says they might save and send the child themselves.'

- 'Another young adult that attended one of the Scripture Union holidays was also given new experiences and opportunities. She was offered to participate in a two-day training course to become a Scripture Union leader. This training/experience would provide this young woman with great future life opportunities.'

- 'L. is a young person who struggles to make the right choices at times. He is easily led and there are concerns about him in the community especially during the summer holidays. He lives with his father who does not keep good health and is unable to spend time with L. participating in activities. This holiday has given L. the opportunity to experience new challenges, make new friends and has given him respite from a caring role. L. said "It was a fantastic holiday and I would like to go again."'

- 'T. returned with more confidence and a very large smile. For T. to be part of the non-judgemental, friendly caring environment the leaders promoted was invaluable in improving her low esteem and emotional well-being ... T. has also had the best experiences of her life.'

Parents

- 'One of the comments my daughter made about Scripture Union which will always stick in my head was the thing that she liked about it, was that nobody was ever left sitting alone. If anybody was alone somebody would go speak to them and bring them into the activities they were doing.'

- 'They (children) came back this year on such a high from the people they were around, the activities they got to do, and all these amazing stories that they would never have been able to do if it wasn't for Prison Fellowship and Circle getting them to Scripture Union camp.'

- 'They (the camps) have totally brought 'my weans' out of their shells and made them more adventurous, more curious. I thank Prison Fellowship, Circle and Scripture Union for all that as well. Thanks very much. Can I just say a big thank you on behalf of my two wonderful boys .... they said they loved it and had lots of cool fun .... It was the first time they had both been away from home and their Mum .... they said it was great and wish they could go back. So thanks a lot for giving my boys a fantastic time. Thank you from me, their Mum, and my boys.'

Young people

- 'Me and A. went to Glenshee. The food was good, and I loved it, thanks to the leaders for keeping us safe, of course, that's your job! A special thanks to Morrison for making us laugh. The raft building activity was my favourite. The trip to Perth was good but it was boring when we had to go because I enjoyed the swimming. I made lots of nice things for my step-dad, my mum and my sister. I made four new friends.'

- 'I went on holiday to Lendrick Muir. We all went to Glasgow to get the bus. It's the first time my Gran let me go without a big person. When I got there, I felt like a princess going into a castle! We got a room with four of us – it was good fun. Ruth was great. We walked to church on Sunday; the deer were big. We talked about God and sang a lot. I liked singing and the stories. I made a lot of friends and did a lot of fun things like climbing a big tree with a blindfold on! I also did go-karts, bungee jumps, swimming and camped out all night! I love to sing. I think my Gran had a good time without all of us.'

- 'I enjoyed all the holiday, meeting new friends and had a good break away when I needed it most. Everything was fantastic. Thank you. I would just like to stress how much I enjoyed Scripture Union. It was so much fun. I got to meet such amazing and inspirational people and made lots of new friends that I hope to stay in touch with 'forever' and I'm so thankful for it.'

- 'I liked all of it as I made lots of friends and enjoyed all the activities.'

- 'Everyone there was so amazing ... the cooks were fantastic every meal was amazing thanks to them (except the soup which I don't like) but I tried something new – TACOS they were FANDABIDOSEY'

- 'Lendrick Muir .... doing the different activities like high ropes and go-karting.'

- 'I give it 20 out of 10.' I didn't dislike anything I loved it all it was so good. I would go back anytime.'

- 'C. stated that she really loved the holiday. She enjoyed the slides, abseiling, gorge walking, speed boats and pony trekking. The food was good and the leaders were very nice. She met lots of nice people at the camp.'

- 'A. stated that the staff were really good, the activities were really good and they didn't have a lot of free time, which was great and much better. Although she has enjoyed her holidays at Lendrick Muir the last two years she felt the activities at Kingscross were much better and both girls took part in all the activities. A. did comment on how it was uncomfortable lying in sleeping bags and would have much preferred a camp bed. A also felt that the tents were really cramped and they had nowhere to put their clothes. Despite being bitten by cleggs and spending the night in hospital, she said that it was a great holiday!'

- 'T. loved the talent show, she said she enjoyed the staff taking part, it was good fun. The only thing she didn't like, was that the holiday came to an end and she wished it could have gone on forever.'

- 'L. said there was nothing he didn't like about it. He had been very upset because he didn't think he was going to get there due to arriving too early. He said he liked it all.'

- 'L. said she had been very nervous about going and right up until going on the bus talked about not going. However, she cried when it was time to come home. She made new friends and has continued to meet up with these friends.'

Christmas Gifts

Christmas can be a difficult time for families, especially when they are separated from each other, when the breadwinner is not around, and when financial hardship is the daily experience. Christmas can become a stressful, pressurised time, rather than a happy celebration of 'Good News, of great joy for everyone'. So, the other major part of the Angel Tree programme is building the family bonds by ensuring that parents in prison have a gift to give to their children at Christmas. Listen to this lovely feedback:

- 'Everyone who requested a present came down, received their presents and wrapped them. They were all appreciative of receiving them saying how delighted their kids will be ... a big thank you from them.'

- '... a total of twenty-eight families and fifty-one children received gifts. All the children received at least two gifts directly from the person they were visiting, and the gifts were given to the prisoners to distribute prior to them going into the visit room. We also provided twelve families who were not able to attend the parties with gifts, which were all gratefully received. We even received a thank you card, even being posted to us from one thankful family ... All of the children were delighted to get gifts from their loved one and in particular from their Mums and Dads ....'

- 'The Family Contact Office would like to say a "BIG THANK YOU" to all of the very kind people who donated Christmas gifts to the children of prisoners.'

- 'Year after year you have continued to support us and by doing so, have managed to bring some cheer to those who otherwise may be finding it difficult to cope at this time.'

- 'We have aimed to ensure that every child who visits the establishment is given a gift and have allowed their father to present it to them.'

- 'This has given both the prisoner and their child a brief sense of normality and has provided a few additional smiles within the visit room!'

- 'The prisoners have shown much appreciation and some have been overwhelmed by the gift their child has received.'

- 'Please thank all the very generous individuals who gave to Barlinnie and wish them a Merry Christmas and a Peaceful New Year. Kindest Regards, Carol, Emma and David, Barlinnie Family Contact Office.'

CHAPTER 8

'A Time to Write'

The 'A Time to Write' Letter Writing Programme is a new project which PFS started working on in the summer of 2020 as part of our response to the Coronavirus pandemic. In recent years there has been greater awareness of the level of isolation and loneliness experienced by men and women in Scottish prisons. In a recent survey, over 50 per cent of those prisoners who are over fifty years old, in HMP Edinburgh, said that they received no visits. We recognised that this sense of isolation had increased even more during the pandemic, as the men and women in prison had spent even more time in their cells.

The name was chosen by one of the prison chaplains, recognising that both volunteers and those in prison have time to write, and also the sense of opportunity that the pandemic has presented to develop new initiatives to reduce isolation and loneliness among prisoners.

'A Time to Write' is a monitored letter-writing project, in which Prison Fellowship volunteers are linked up with men and women in Scottish Prisons and commit to writing regular letters to these individuals. Letters are written on a monthly basis by volunteers who have to complete a training programme. Letters are sent through the PFS office to ensure no personal details are passed on.

The letter-writing manual was written with input from the Scottish Prison Service, and forms the basis of our training programme. Referrals are generated by chaplains who will promote the programme in the prisons in which they work. Men and women in these prisons will then fill out a form asking to be part of the programme. The form is then passed on to Prison Fellowship Scotland and a letter writer is paired with the prisoner concerned.

The purpose of this project is to relieve isolation and provide care and support to men and women who are lonely and/or vulnerable and who may not have any friends or family or outside contact, whilst they are in prison. This isolation is recognised as being a key factor in the poor mental health of those in prison, something that is of major concern to the Scottish Prison Service and their encouragement has been a key driver in setting up this project. We also recognise that in PFS, we have a motivated group of volunteers who are keen to do more. As our work has grown, we have become aware that there are a significant number of volunteers who cannot support our in-prison work because they live in more remote areas, and the regular travel to prison would be too much.

At the time of writing it has been agreed that a pilot project will run in four Scottish prisons: HMP Edinburgh, HMP Cornton Vale, HMP Glenochil and HMYOI Polmont and we have just linked our first volunteer with a man in prison in Edinburgh. These prisons hold a mixture of prisoners ranging from women prisoners in Cornton Vale, a prison population that is recognised as having very little connection with the outside world, to an older population in Glenochil and Edinburgh. The Scottish Prison Service was also keen to include Young Offenders in the pilot project who are looked after in HMYOI Polmont.

CHAPTER 9

Professional Voices

We are an unusual organisation, in that most of our work is done inside another organisation i.e. The Scottish Prison Service, so the voices of the chaplains and governors we work for, and the staff we work beside, as well as the observations of Her Majesty's Inspectors of Prisons in Scotland, are important for us and we are grateful that we enjoy good relations with, and the co-operation of, the SPS.

Their comments on our work are critical. These are very important voices for PFS.

The Chaplain's Voice

All Prison Fellowship groups operate as part of the work and under the supervision of Chaplains. As well as PFS training, our volunteers are trained by the Scottish Prison Service Chaplaincy Advisers. Their encouragement and advice facilitate our work.

Rev. Martin Forrest, Chaplain HMP Low Moss

'The new HMP Low Moss opened in March 2012, housing over 700 long-term, short-term and remand adult male prisoners. The relationship with Prison Fellowship Scotland was established right at the start and PFS volunteers have been working alongside the ecumenical, multi-faith team of six chaplains ever since.

One set of volunteers runs a fellowship meeting every Monday evening with a very varied programme including speakers, DVDs and discussion on a wide range of topics, always starting with a very popular time of prayer and song. This same team, with a few additions and subtractions, has faithfully turned up every Monday night and led a very cheerful, relaxed meeting, which has been enjoyed and appreciated by what seems like several 'generations' or 'waves' of prisoners over the past seven years. The men like the content of the evenings but just as important to them, is the company of the volunteers who, the men know, give up their own time to do this – and they always say how grateful they are to have this time of fellowship with the 'Good, decent Christian people who give their time to be with us'.

Another, equally enthusiastic group of volunteers runs the Wednesday afternoon Sycamore Tree course. This is a voluntary course, but it has effectively become a staple part of the offence-related programme that Low Moss has to offer. The volunteers have now run thirty-four Sycamore courses with nearly 300 prisoners successfully completing the course over the past seven years. An indication of the success of the course is that we have not had to advertise it or push it for years. By the end of every course we already have more than enough names for the next course, or two, and almost every participant now says that they heard about it, not from a chaplain or any other member of staff, but from a fellow prisoner.

The partnership between Prison Fellowship and the chaplains at Low Moss has been a very successful one and the chaplains are extremely grateful to all the PF volunteers for their fellowship and their hard work. They have all hugely enriched what the chaplaincy has to offer to the men in Low Moss, and their faithfulness and dedication has been a powerful witness to staff and prisoners alike.'

Rev. P Jill Clancy, Chaplain HMP Barlinnie

'Since joining the prison community, first as a part-time chaplain in HMP Kilmarnock, and now as a full-time chaplain working in HMP Barlinnie, I can only say that I have the utmost respect for Prison Fellowship Scotland and their work in both prisons.

Actually my connection with them started way back around 1991, when I was a Training in Evangelism student, and a small group of us joined Prison Fellowship in HMP Glenochil to sing and share with the men there, and then when I became minister in Gourock. I joined the Prison Fellowship Group in HMP Greenock on a couple of occasions, sharing with them my own story of faith. So, whether it was sharing in the fellowship groups or indeed being part of the group by attending the Sycamore Tree course, I have valued the work and commitment that Prison Fellowship has in sharing the gospel message with those who seek the Lord while in prison.

There is no doubt that the prisoners look forward to the groups – there they feel safe, there they love to sing, pray and they especially enjoy the tea, coffee and biscuits. To be honest I think that is a bit of a highlight. But in the group, they are accepted, loved and there is always a strong message from the Word of God. So they learn and grow and hopefully, draw closer to their Creator God in these times of fellowship.

I also know that the men the leaders come into contact with week by week are not forgotten about when they leave the prison. I know that they are prayed for and remembered. The men and women, also know that, although they may feel a little ashamed if they return to prison, they are still welcomed again and again back to the groups where they are not judged, but probably treated like long lost friends.

Chaplaincy Teams are enriched by having a Prison Fellowship group within their prisons and I hope that all prisons continue to value the work that these committed volunteers do. The time they give is very much appreciated.'

The Governor's Voice

Willie Stuart, Governor HMP Shotts

'During my time working in various establishments across the SPS, I have always found the input provided by Prison Fellowship to be a welcomed, additional contribution to the management of those in our care. Prison Fellowship brings a friendly face, a listening ear along with, a supportive non-judgemental approach, sometimes even providing a chocolate biscuit, all of which allows those attending their session an opportunity to relax and discuss subjects of a spiritual and secular nature. Often seen about establishments, speaking to individuals and groups in the residential areas, and providing a range of church services in partnership with SPS chaplains. They also make a significant contribution to challenging offending via the Sycamore Tree course, which allows those they work with to explore the impact of their criminality on others, wider communities and their own lives. A group of individuals who are dedicated to their work and a pleasure to work alongside within our prisons.'

The Inspector's Voice

Rev. Andrew McLellan, Chief Inspector of Prisons 2002–2009

'No doubt much has changed in prisons and in Prison Fellowship, since I finished my time inspecting prisons over ten years ago. But two things unhappily remain the same: prison overcrowding and public attitudes to prisoners. I saw Prison Fellowship do very valuable work to combat the effects of prison overcrowding; and I know that they made a real contribution to changing public attitudes. Now, as much as ever, in these two fields, Prison Fellowship is very much needed.

In the last few years, prison overcrowding dropped a little, as prisoner numbers dropped a little. But very recently the trend has been reversed and the numbers have crept up, and overcrowding has crept up. Why does this matter? What can Prison Fellowship do about it?

I once listed "Nine Evils of Overcrowding":

1. It increases the likelihood of cell-sharing: two people, often complete strangers, are required to live in very close proximity. This will involve another person who may have a history of violence, of whose medical and mental health history the prisoner will know nothing, and it will involve sharing a toilet.

2. It increases noise and tension.

3. It increases the number of prisoners managed by prison staff who, as a result, have less time to devote to screening prisoners for self-harm or suicide, prisoners with mental health problems and prisoners who are potentially violent.

4. It increases the availability of drugs since there are more people who want drugs, and prison staff have less time to search.

5. It makes it likely that prisoners will have less access to staff; and that they will find that those staff whom they do access will have less time to deal with them.

6. The resources in prison will be more stretched, so prisoners will have less access to programmes, education, training, work etc.

7. Facilities will also be more stretched so that laundry will be done less often and food quality will deteriorate.

8. Prisoners will spend more time in their cells.

9. Family contact and visits will be restricted.

Everyone who cares about prisons should care about these things. Every one of them makes things worse for everybody. There is nothing that Prison Fellowship can do about some of them, but there is a good deal that Prisons Fellowship has done, and will continue to do, to diminish the harm caused by others.

For example, the last on the list, the restriction in family contact, is very damaging. There is evidence that good family contact is very important in reducing reoffending. So the work of Prison Fellowship with the families of prisoners becomes increasingly significant when overcrowded prisons do not provide the kind of family contact which is needed. Prison Fellowship cannot make visits happen when a prison is unable to provide the necessary staff, but Prison Fellowship does work with the families of prisoners, and any such work will help family relationships. Think of the summer holidays for children. Think of the gifts at Christmas. Anything Prison Fellowship can do to support the families of prisoners helps prisoners and helps family relationships.

Or take, from the list above of the evils of overcrowding, the importance of access to programmes. There are many programmes provided in prisons to help prisoners change, and some of them are very good. I don't remember seeing a better programme than the Sycamore Tree Course. Prison Fellowship describes this as "a restorative justice programme delivered inside prison looking at offending and the impact on victims, promoting the need to accept responsibility for their actions". As the name suggests, it is a programme which emerges from the Biblical story of Zacchaeus and Jesus. I remember the warmest of tributes to the course from prisoners and from prison staff alike.

There is nothing that Prison Fellowship can do to reduce prison overcrowding, but Prison Fellowship certainly succeeds in reducing the harm that prison overcrowding causes. Every one of the evils of overcrowding increases the level of stress in a prison. Violence and fear and sometimes suicide are often the companions of high-stress levels. Who can calculate the difference Prison Fellowship can make in a stress-filled prison? The difference Prison Fellowship can make with a listening ear, a kind word, a calming presence, a message of faith?

Public attitudes to prisoners also seem to have changed very little in the ten years since I stopped inspecting prisons. I have no statistical evidence for saying this, but every time I hear a radio phone-in programme about imprisonment, I am convinced of it. Not only is it the same things that listeners are saying about prisoners, it often seems to be the very same people who were phoning into the same programmes ten years ago and more!

You know the sort of thing – "Flat-screen TV indeed" (as if you could buy any other kind); "Holiday camp"; "Hotel"; "The best of food"; "everything has gone soft". Sometimes on inspections I took with me someone who had never been in prison before. Always the comment was the same, "I did not realise that prison life was so bleak". Yet people who have never been inside a jail dominate the airways and dominate the comments to the press, and people who seek to offer a more informed view are dismissed as bleeding hearts.

We could do with more bleeding hearts and we could do with more do-gooders. We could do with more people who know what imprisonment is really like. Demands for harsher punishments and more brutal prison conditions are never going to bring about a safer, gentler Scotland. Prisons must be allowed to do what they are supposed to do: they must be allowed to engage in the extremely difficult process of helping criminals turn away from a life of crime. Only when public opinion understands the importance of human approaches to prisons, will Scotland become a safer place.

So the work of Prison Fellowship is vital. For Prison Fellowship has a foot in both camps. It is rooted inside prisons and it is welcomed inside prisons, but it is also placed firmly in the world outside. Its great strength is its large number of volunteers, who live and work in the real world. In their daily life and conversations, they are able to change people's minds about the reality of imprisonment. At their work and at their play and in their homes, they are in a position to make clear the real needs of prisoners and the real needs of prison staff. By being there, by their very presence, Prison Fellowship volunteers make the conversation more decent and humane.

Not only that – it is good to hear of Prison Fellowship developing as a force for advocacy, engaging with the Scottish Government, engaging with the Scottish Prison Service and keeping in the forefront concepts of justice and forgiveness, which have their roots in the Bible. At the same time, Prison Fellowship continues to do what it has always done – to pray regularly and faithfully for all the needs of those involved in different ways in the prison system. All of this helping to make things better.

More than a century ago Winston Churchill said in the House of Commons:

> The mood and temper of the public in regard to the treatment of crime and criminals is one of the most unfailing tests of the civilisation of any country. A calm and dispassionate recognition of the rights of the accused against the state, and even of convicted criminals against the state, a constant heart-searching by all charged with the duty of punishment, a desire and eagerness to rehabilitate in the world of industry all those who have paid their dues in the hard coinage of punishment, tireless efforts towards the discovery of curative and regenerating processes, and an unfaltering faith that there is a treasure, if only you can find it, in the heart of every person – these are the symbols which in the treatment of crime and criminals mark and measure the stored-up strength of a nation, and are the sign and proof of the living virtue in it.

If he was right, and I believe he was, then thank goodness for Prison Fellowship. Thank goodness for Prison Fellowship working to make more civilised the mood and temper of the public in regard to the treatment of crime and criminals; and thank goodness for Prison

Fellowship with its unfaltering faith that there is a treasure, if only you can find it, in the heart of every person. That is exactly what is needed.'

David Strang, HM Chief Inspector of Prisons for Scotland 2013–2018

'As HM Chief Inspector of Prisons for Scotland, I had the privilege of inspecting the fifteen prisons in Scotland on a regular basis. My duties were to inspect and report on the conditions in prison and the treatment of the men and women who were held there. During the course of my five years as HM Chief Inspector, I met a wide range of people who contributed to our inspection findings. Most important were the people who were detained in prison; it was their voice I particularly wanted to hear. For many people, prison is a bleak and harsh place to be. Few would choose to spend any time as a prisoner – it was not what they would have chosen for their life.

Many people told me about the pain they felt as a result of their incarceration. They realised that they had damaged many people, including the victims of the crimes they had committed. Many also felt they had let down their partner or family and were now separated from those they wished to love and care for. Broken relationships were a common feature of the lives of people in prison, many of them having suffered at the hands of others in their earlier years. Too many men and women told me of their despair and hopelessness, feeling that they had made a mess of their lives and were not confident that there was a different path their lives could take. Loneliness, isolation, guilt and fear were commonly expressed emotions.

Society expects people, who have served a prison sentence, to change their ways and to return to their community as responsible citizens. For many people this is much more easily said than done. There are many obstacles put in the way of people trying to reintegrate back into society, particularly after a long sentence in prison. Some will have no accommodation to return to, others will be unable to find employment because of the stigma and distrust attached to someone who has served a prison sentence. Many people in prison have serious mental health and addiction problems.

This rather bleak view is only part of the picture. I also met men and women who had had a more positive experience of their time in prison. For some, it provided an opportunity to make a fresh start and to put behind them the harmful behaviours of the past. I was impressed with many of the staff and other people working in prisons, who invested in the lives of people in prison, to support them on their journey and to assist them to make the changes they wished to. The Scottish Prison Service has a stated aim to 'Unlock Potential and Transform Lives'. There are numerous examples where the support available to people in prison has enabled them to set out on a new and positive journey at the end of their sentence.

One group of people who have supported transformational change in the lives of men and women in prison are the volunteers belonging to Prison Fellowship Scotland. PFS members (volunteers) regularly attend prisons across Scotland to encourage and support men and women in prison. Their faithful service means a great deal to the people in prison who attend the regular PFS meetings. They particularly value the quality of the relationships and the different nature of their interactions. PFS volunteers are not an official part of the prison hierarchy. They bring a supportive and non-judgemental approach and are seen as being 'on their side'. Above all, they bring encouragement that change and transformation are possible. The arrangements for worship and fellowship in a safe place is a highly valued opportunity in what can otherwise feel a threatening environment.

PFS links in well with others working in the prison and in the community. They always work alongside the chaplaincy team and have many positive contacts with other third sector and charity organisations in the community who can support people when they leave prison. In several prisons, PFS runs The Sycamore Tree course, which is a highly valued course that addresses issues of forgiveness and transformation.

At a deep level, PFS can support people who are feeling lost and broken, encouraging transformation through a new identity and sense of belonging. They are known for their regular attendance and have a reputation for sticking with people and standing alongside them on what can often be a difficult journey. Above all, they bring a message of hope and an encouragement that a person's current situation is not all that their life can be.'

A Prison Officer's Voice
David Hyslop, Residential Officer

'I have now been a residential prison officer for twenty-eight years and worked with all prisoners, both male and female. Many of these days have been challenging and difficult. The role of Prison Fellowship for me has been a relief from a challenging day that allows prisoners to drop the image, which has to be portrayed to staff, and gives them an opportunity to relax and reflect. Many prisoners wait all week for the Prison Fellowship meeting – getting excited from the moment the request is placed, usually commenting on a number of occasions, "Am I down for the Fellowship?" and "Make sure I'm opened up", this is both relevant to the men and women alike.

This excitement is particularly evident amongst the female population who always attend in large numbers. They like to get away from the noise of the banging doors and the shouting. They can feel a little bit of normal life, chatting, having tea, singing and hearing stories that are particularly relevant to them about changing their life for the better.

Many do not attend formal Church services but come to the Fellowship for the warmth and acceptance. I have had comments like, "They are really lovely people" and "...can't wait for the next meeting". For me, this is particularly noticeable for some prisoners who are difficult for us to manage on a daily basis. They can be quieter and indeed more reflective.

I have known the Prison Fellowship volunteers for over twenty years. I cannot fault their dedication and commitment to change people's lives and give a hopeful outlook.'

CHAPTER 10

Liberated Voices

There is a phenomenon called 'jail Christianity', where a man or woman in prison is enthusiastic about faith, but when they are released and are back again into stressful or chaotic environments without the support they need, their faith, either gradually or quickly, disappears. That is why it is a real encouragement to see men and women continuing in their faith when they leave prison; having the emotional and spiritual strength and the practical support to put their lives back together, enabling them to make their own contribution in society and in the church. As you read you will see that for some, it has been a tough and rocky road and that many of those in our prisons are as much sinned against as sinners!

These are the voices of those who have left prison behind:

J. 'I love the following quotation from the Bible in Genesis 39:20-23.

"While Joseph was there in the prison, the Lord was with him; he showed him kindness and granted him favour in the eyes of the prison warden. So the warden put Joseph in charge of all those held in the prison, and he was made responsible for all that was done there. The warden paid no attention to anything under Joseph's care, because the Lord was with Joseph and gave him success in whatever he did." It will become clear why ....

My parents were newlywed teenagers when I came along. Dad worked every hour he could in a local factory, and fixed cars at the side of the house at night, to top up the household income. Mum worked whatever part-time jobs she could get – a seamstress at the hosiery, school cleaner in the mornings, and cleaning a local hotel in the evening. Ours was never a religious home. We had traditional working-class values and we wanted for nothing. Like most families we had our fair share of difficulties, but it was a home filled with love.

From start to finish I found school very difficult. Bullying was rife, and there was very little the teachers could do about it. Even at five years old, I felt like I didn't fit. I couldn't connect and struggled to belong. I wasn't tough, and I felt like I was destined for trouble from day one.

My first brush with the law was at the age of eight. I remember "rescuing" an abandoned bicycle from the street. I didn't know any better and took it for a spin. The police pulled me over on the street to question me. I had committed my first crime: "theft by finding". When my mum noticed me talking to the police, she shouted me over and told me, "Don't you ever talk to the police! We don't trust or talk to them". The one thing that was considered worse than a criminal was a "grass" – another word for a police informer.

Through primary school I got into lots of trouble. I was given the strap regularly. One time I was belted for a playground misdemeanour by the head teacher. My hands were bruised and blistered, right up my wrists, and I went home crying. My mum took me straight back round to the school and threatened the head teacher, "If you ever hit my son again, I'll come back and hit you!" Even when I was in the wrong my mum stood up for me. I think she influenced my view of authority.

Despite struggling with school, one primary school teacher really engaged me by using the story of "Joseph and the Amazing Technicolour Dreamcoat". I vividly remember how inspired I was by the Bible story of this young lad rejected by his brothers. Joseph was betrayed, sold into slavery, and ended up in prison. Right there he experienced the God working for his good. Something about this dreamer reminded me of myself. It was like the story of Joseph pointed me towards a special value in my own life that I couldn't see. I think that teacher saw it in me, and all her other pupils. It came to mean so much more to me years later. I found myself able to identify with the young, misunderstood lad filled with potential, who found the grace and favour of God in the darkest of prison cells.

During those younger years, my friends and I often visited the Gospel Hall in Anderson Drive on a Thursday night for the "Happy Hour". We learned some catchy choruses like "Deep and Wide", "The Countdown's Getting Lower Every Day", and "Zacchaeus Was a Very Little Man". The Bible stories always pointed us towards Jesus. To be honest, we had ulterior motives for attending. If anyone had a birthday, they would receive a bar of chocolate and everyone would sing Happy Birthday. Needless to say, we had more than our fair share of birthdays! I think the folks in the Gospel Hall knew fine well we were chancers, but they were very kind and indulged us with love ... and chocolate!

When I went to secondary school, my reputation went ahead of me. I was surrounded by others in the same predicament. What made everything worse, was the rumour that I was gay. This was the early 80s and homophobia was rife. I wasn't gay, but despite that I was ridiculed and bullied; surrounded and hounded; spat upon; beaten up; excluded from friendship groups; and searched for money for most of my teenage years. "Find-keep-break-jaw" was the name for the regular routine of being stop-searched for lunch money. These years were traumatic, and I had no idea how to process it at the time.

My brushes with the law went from bad to worse. I was suspended from school on numerous occasions. I had social workers all through my secondary years, and along with teachers, they tried to help me as best they could. One guidance teacher came to speak on my family's behalf at a Children's Hearing. She pleaded with the Panel not to send me to a children's home. She testified to my parent's positive influence and promised to do her best to help me finish school. She did help me, and I scraped through my exams. I failed them all, but I gave them a go. The support of this teacher would prove to be significant later. Oh, the benefit of hindsight!

I left school as soon as I turned sixteen. I also left home and spent a year sleeping between friends' couches and lofts, ducking and diving here and there. All this time my mum and dad were going through a divorce and my mum had major surgery on her spine. This ended her working life at thirty-four.

I smoked and swallowed, sniffed and drank, any substance for a high. I shoplifted and broke into sheds and houses to make pocket money. At the age of seventeen I was arrested, taken to court and jailed. No bravado or pretending then. It was a jolt to my system. My first stop was HM Longriggend Remand Institution where I spent four weeks, each day under twenty-three hour lock-up. I was just a kid – the same age as my mum when she had me. I felt suicidal and struggled to cope with the isolation. When I was sentenced to spend most of the next year in prison, I started off in the detention centre, HMP Glenochil Young Offenders Institution (YOI). The ethos at that time was "short-sharp-shock". No privileges, no smoking, a hardcore fitness regime, marching daily and shoes polished to a mirror – like sheen – imagine military boot camp for teenagers. After a month in Glenochil I received my yellow grade and applied for trusted prisoner status (D-category). I was successful and moved to the open prison, HMP Castle Huntly YOI near Dundee, to serve the rest of my sentence. This move would change everything for me. I had more opportunities to socialise and did daily work including cleaning and gardening. During this time everything changed.

One night another inmate invited me to the Prison Fellowship group. I went along not knowing what to expect. The people were kind and seemed genuinely pleased to be there. They said it was because God loved us. I remember the simple Gospel message the Prison Chaplain shared that night. He drew a valley – and called it "the valley of sin". We're all in this valley of sin, and we're stuck, trapped – and that's true for everyone whether they're in prison or outside. The things we do that hurt ourselves and others, our broken hopes and dreams, all come from our broken relationship with God. We try to scramble out of this valley, to get on in life, but time and again we slip back into sin. We could easily identify with that as prisoners. The Bible says in Romans 3:23 – "All have sinned and fall short of the glory of God." I knew that to be true. It was my experience. We were all made to live in the glory of God, and I was far from it. No one in the Prison Fellowship group judged us. They shared this message with kindness.

The Chaplain then drew another valley, and he called that the valley of death with the simple message – we will all die but because

Jesus rose again, we too can be lifted out of the valley of death. The amazing thing about all this is that we can't do anything to earn it. We can't do anything to deserve eternal life. It's a free gift, and all we can do is receive it, by faith – and that's what I did that very night I heard the simple Gospel in HMP Castle Huntly. The Chaplain led me in a very simple prayer of saying sorry to God, declaring my belief in Jesus' death and resurrection, and asking for complete forgiveness and a new life. I became a Christian. I was given a Bible to read, and the first thing I was encouraged to do was tell somebody. I told everybody.

My life and behaviour changed, and I had a new hope. I felt joy again for the first time in a long time. Was it easy, plain sailing? No, it wasn't. In fact, the biggest challenge came next. Did I mean it? Was I serious? As soon as I left prison, just a month after praying a simple prayer to ask Jesus to come into my life, I was tested. And the truth is, I failed. I turned away from God to live my own way again. Old habits kicked back in – lying, cheating, stealing, drugs, alcohol and violence. Eighteen months later I found myself in a real mess. I was taken into psychiatric care with drug-induced psychosis through the prolonged pressure of addiction, devastated relationships, bereavement, hurt, and criminality. And that's when I hit rock bottom. I called out to God again and He heard my cry.

I called the Prison Chaplain who had explained Jesus' Good News to me and he prayed with me in Castle Huntly. He helped me connect with a local church minister who prayed for me, helped me understand the Good News and showed me how it worked out in practice. This is what I missed out on when I was first released from prison. Things began to turn around, gradually, but surely. Over the following six months I would be healed of my mental health problems, saved from homelessness and unemployment, and able to put thieving hands to meaningful work. Where there were broken relationships in my family, I sought reconciliation, even making amends with sworn enemies who couldn't believe the change in my life. Where I had done wrong in my local community I apologised. As far as I could, I put things right. God was showing me what it looked like with His help to clean up my mess. This included ending an unhealthy relationship and becoming celibate until God led me later in life into Christian marriage. Within a year I emerged from crippling debt and was able to make restitution for things that I had stolen.

While I was working full time, I went back to night school to sit Higher English. In my creative writing piece, I shared my story about becoming a Christian and wrote a book review of *The Cross and the Switchblade* by David Wilkerson. I received a D, which wasn't great, but it was the best academic achievement I had attained to date. It enabled me to apply for Bible College, where I would spend the next four years working towards an honours degree in Theology, which I completed with flying colours!

During my four years at Bible College I married the love of my life, Yvonne. Twenty years later, we have four beautiful kids and two decades of faith-filled adventure. Never in my most lucid moments did I believe I would be able to make such progress. But deep down within me there was a dream from God that, like Joseph, I was of immense worth and value, and that life was supposed to be better. I was meant to be something more than a troublesome lad. I began to truly believe in the plans God had for me, and door after door opened up for me to speak to others, to travel and work, and create and bless, and be blessed. I dedicated my life to serving and reaching out to others with the Good News of Jesus, and this included becoming a Prison Fellowship volunteer. As a result I've spent a lot of time in prison since becoming a Christian – much more than I ever did when I was a young offender.

When I graduated from Bible College, I was offered a scholarship to do a post-graduate diploma in alcohol and drug studies. I studied hard, graduated again, and became an addictions worker in my home town. From there I went on to work for a group of churches to set up an alcohol-free nightclub that reached out to hundreds of young people every week. And then from nightclub manager to pastor – I was called into local church ministry. I now lead a vibrant church in Bishopbriggs. These things are way beyond what I could ever imagine God would do in my life. God is so good! He is able to do exceedingly, abundantly, above and beyond all we could ever ask or imagine.

I will share with you just one more story. I was part of a summer holiday club with my church. One day during lunch a lady came into the church hall. She stood at the doorway and looked straight at me. I didn't know who it was at first. She looked at me and exclaimed "J., is that you?" It was the teacher who came to the Children's Panel to speak up for me and support my parents, when I was a young lad in high school. She asked me, "What happened to you?" "And here I was, all these years later. I told her my story and how I had become a Christian. With tears streaming down her face, she said to me, "I prayed for you every day." I was gobsmacked, and so was she. But this was a wonderful demonstration of the power of prayer. This lady prayed for me and many of my peers, and many of them have also become Christians. Hallelujah!'

D. 'I attended different Prison Fellowship groups in different jails. The first one I attended was in HMP Barlinnie which was a fellowship group very early on in my journey with God. For me, it was a place of peace. I could go with like-minded people, who mostly believed what I was discovering. It was a place to worship God and learn more about Him.

From Barlinnie I was transferred to HMP Kilmarnock, where I continued to attend the groups. I was beginning to grow more in my faith and become more committed to learning about it. I spent another six months there attending church and Fellowship. The relationships I was building with the volunteers would play a key part in my journey and in my life changing. We would discuss topics such as faith, and it was a really safe environment to ask questions – even if they were a bit off the chart! This is where I responded to the call to follow Jesus.

For me, one of the most important parts of being part of the Prison Fellowship group was when I was released. The volunteers keeping in touch with me, meeting with me and praying for me etc. was a huge encouragement. They helped me find a church near where I lived and thankfully I ended up finding and becoming part of the church I currently now lead in. God brought many people into my life who were influencing and helping me, as the difficulties of life and doubts would arise in me. I am grateful to God.'

I. 'I became a Christian when I was fifteen-years-old. It was a genuine step of faith, towards Jesus Christ, into a Christian church that would absorb the next seven years of my life. At age twenty I married and the week after we returned from honeymoon, I commenced psychiatric nurse training. One year after our marriage I became a dad.

The nature of the training was all about self-development. Eventually, in questioning everything I believed, I chose to walk away from the church. Sadly, most of the 150 people I'd spent my last formative years with and who had become family, judged me to have abandoned them or so it seemed, cutting me out of their lives. In becoming wholly absorbed with myself and my own needs, I chose to walk away from all responsibility. I'd felt very hurt by being so judged that, at the time, I remember vowing to myself that I would never allow another human being to hurt me in the way I felt abandoned by those people. Sadly, I was also abandoning my own wife and daughter. I qualified as a Registered Mental Nurse and moved to the south coast of England to party, and explore the person I wanted to become.

Over the next decade or so I would repeat the same patterns – moving from job to job, city to city, relationship to relationship. A man on the run. As soon as I felt a person was getting too close, or if the pressure of life was becoming too complex, off I'd go, creating new start after new start. I made a huge success of detaching myself from any relationships that might ultimately cause me pain.

Periodically I would dip my toe in the water of church attendance. But, in order to maintain my vow, this had to remain infrequent. At some point in this hedonistic lifestyle, I crossed the point of controlling alcohol and failed to notice that it was now controlling me. I was so far down a path of isolation, I knew of no way back. I was one step away from total self-destruction. It was exactly where Satan, the destroyer and liar, had wanted me to be. The inevitable consequence of so much unresolved pain and running, culminated in the criminal actions that led me into a custodial sentence, with a punishment part of four years – I would spend a total of 18+ years in prison.

Very early on in my sentence, I heard about Prison Fellowship. Those "happy-clappy" Christians were definitely to be avoided! From a safe distance, I noticed how faithful in their commitment they were – that their love and support seemed unconditional, much like God's love for me. Even though I would dip in and out of Fellowship, depending on my own level of pain at the time, the volunteers were always gracious and glad to see me return. I thank God for the love, and practical support, over the years, from Prison Fellowship volunteers in HMP Greenock, HMP Barlinnie, HMP Low Moss PF team of volunteers and the Chaplains there. They were sowing seeds of love in my life, which would eventually bear fruit. As the years rolled by, and as I attempted to somehow deal with, or understand, all that prison was throwing at me, I was gradually able to return to my first love in Jesus Christ. I was more able to accept full responsibility for the consequences of my own actions and, slowly with God's help, I began to learn how to forgive as God healed me.

It was in attending a Monday evening Prison Fellowship meeting, at HMP Low Moss, that God met me in a quietly powerful and life-changing way. He reminded me that when I had become a Christian, all those years ago, He already knew the mess I would make of my life. But He loved me anyhow. That helped me forgive myself. Nothing takes God by surprise. His love is truly unconditional.

Then I had to renounce the vow of making myself an emotional island. I see now that my own words had enslaved me. Be careful what you wish for. I decided to change my mind and open myself to love and healing, to not limit what God would do in my life. At another meeting, there stood a large wooden cross propped up against the wall in the Multi-Faith Centre. In a very low-key manner, we were invited to take things to the cross, in our minds, and to welcome healing. But – and here was the key – we then had to choose NEVER to pick it back up again. I did so that night and God set me free from negative emotions and memories I had carried all of my adult life.

It's interesting now that I look back, from the other side of the razor wire to those tough years – years where I felt such injustice, still being in prison after so many years, and I can see the hand of God in my life. The day I got out God promised "to restore the years the locusts had eaten" and that is exactly what He is doing and, I'm honoured to say, my relationship with PF continues to this day.

S. 'I was once a hopeless, homeless drug addict. I was in prison for serious crime and I served two long-term prison sentences. I did the Sycamore Tree course and I used to go to Prison Fellowship in HMP Addiewell. I met a speaker there just before I was released. This man's life story was like my own life experience – I could really identify with what he was saying. I responded to the invitation to respond to God's love and ask Him into my life. I prayed a very simple prayer. I began crying, but not tears of sadness, tears of joy.

This was what I now know to be an encounter with my Saviour. After release I met with George from Prison Fellowship, who kindly took me to a local church. I saw something different in the people at church. I wanted what they had – an overwhelming peace and joy, and so began my search. I found a spiritual home in another church and found myself getting involved but it wasn't long before my demons had returned, and I was back in my old ways. I quickly found myself back in homeless units and skippering.

I eventually ended up in a serious condition in the hospital suffering from a major infection- endocarditis. Drugs had taken everything from me and nearly my life. As I lay there alone again, I cried out to God, "Please just let me die or HELP". And help He did. One thing I learned is God will never turn His back on us. Before long two people from my church heard I was at death's door and prayed for my healing. These people weren't a coincidence but rather a GOD instance.

I was given hope again. After ten weeks in hospital I was released, but I had nowhere to go. I was going back to the homeless unit. I cried out again, "please God help." Later that day the doctors said I was being kept in over the weekend because the infection had appeared again. On the Monday the housing got me a scatter flat and I didn't have to return to the unit! A few days later after resting at home, I made arrangements to go to church again and I've never looked back.

Since then I've been baptised and have been drug and alcohol-free. I've been given a year's relief from my heart infection and I'm at college studying to become a counsellor. I'm living the life God has planned for me and it's amazing. Anything I've done on my own ended in disaster but not now I have a purpose. I've been back in prison but as a visitor this time, and not a prisoner. I thought my life had ended; well now I know it's just started.'

A. was released from Prison in December 2020

'I was released from prison just before Christmas, an already anxious and busy time for many. Upon my release I grabbed the opportunity to work with Connect to the Community (C2C), which is a Christian-based support charity. I liaised with my worker who equipped me with all the information I needed to reintegrate back into the community. She also reassured me that God would be with me on my journey and I would be ok!

Leading up to my release I was very anxious about possible repercussions and a part of me didn't feel worthy to be given a second chance. Through Prison Fellowship and C2C, and even simply reading the Bible and seeking the Lord into my life, really helped me through. Prison Fellowship has really helped me grow as a person and believe that I am worthy and forgiven.

Since my release I have continued to read my Bible and I was also gifted a book of encouraging verses and prayers, which I now have as part of my daily routine, you could call it. I have also been using YouTube to follow a local church's prayer meetings. Lockdown and release from prison for most would be a daunting experience but I am truly grateful for having the Lord guide me through, and just from putting my trust in the Lord has helped me think more positively about myself, get back into employment and continue to mend relationships with my family.

I would really like to thank all of Prison Fellowship Scotland for believing in me and being such amazing support to me when I needed it most and they are still a firm support to me since my release. Also to C2C – they have been fantastic and I just can't wait to see what God has in store for my future!'

G. full circle

G's Story is interesting because it demonstrates how what has happened to us, affects our attitude and behaviour. It demonstrates the importance of support and people you can trust. It shows that it can take time and continuing support, to feel accepted and re-integrated into normal society. But problems and prison are not the full story – new life is possible.

'As a child I always felt like I was waiting at windows. We lived in the top floor of a tenement building in the Glenburn housing scheme in Paisley. From my small single-glazed bedroom window, I would often see police, gang fights, domestic rows, and all sorts of antisocial but, to my young mind, entertaining activity. Growing up I was the oldest of five and my mother was very young and energetic. She loved us but she was a young attractive woman and was always the life and soul of the party. I actually don't remember calling her mum when I was younger, as she would always insist that I called her "Mhairi", which was her name, and we had very much a big-sister-little-brother type relationship.

My mum tried hard with me, and she instilled a morality in me and my brother and sisters in relation to people, racism, bigotry and things like that she did not tolerate. For all she did not get right, this was an ethos that, as a family, we all had and still carry to this day. It couldn't have been easy being a single mother in the middle of a packed housing scheme. We always had men at the door, and we were often babysat by local girls who were "skipping" school. Our house was party central, so I saw a lot as a young boy. It was actually quite fun at times, as I would get money from drunk people wanting to impress my Mum! One weekend, we returned home to find out our regular babysitter's boyfriend had been stabbed and killed during one of these parties. It was in the local paper. On another occasion, a man, pretending to be from the council, chapped our neighbour's door only to shoot him in the face when he opened up the door trustingly. It's fair to say our street was very eventful.

At weekends I would go to see my dad and would often be looked after by my grandmother (my dad's mum) when my dad was out. My grandmother was very affectionate and very loving and I'm very grateful for her input to this day, but once again as a child I found myself constantly waiting at the window for Dad to come home. I remember desperately wanting my dad's approval and validation and using a little boy's logic to try and get it. I thought, "If I pester him more, if I talk to him more, or if I ask him more questions, he will open up to me". I grew up feeling like I was just an annoyance to him. In hindsight I have begun to understand. My father suffered a horrific injury when he got his hand caught in a printing press at his work, and had the tips of his fingers severed. He was stuck for four hours and was very lucky to survive. He was actually in a lot of pain for years ...

I always hung about with guys older than me and was keen to experiment with new drugs or new experiences to try and prove myself. This awakened a chronically addictive personality at a young age. I always worked and I enjoyed having money in my pocket, and I enjoyed the satisfaction of a day's work. I would do paper runs, milk runs, sell football coupons round the neighbours' doors as well as macaroon, tablet etc. Anything to make a few bucks. I started dabbling with heroin after being unwittingly asked to hand out large quantities of the drug, by two well-known gangsters one evening. I had been standing at a phone box when they asked me to "Jump in and help us with a wee message". We travelled to Glasgow in a white Sierra Cosworth with black and blue tiger stripes – the most indiscreet car a criminal could own! I was sent into a close to pick up a large package, then driven round various locations dropping it off in smaller quantities. I was simply the fall guy carrying the stuff in case the car got pulled over by police, but in my mind I was accepted by these two men and I enjoyed the validation I was receiving from them, albeit it was clearly false, as I was simply being manipulated. My reward for helping them was to be taken up to a back road in the Glenniffer Braes and they let me try the drug (heroin) for the first time. I was fifteen-years-old. The validation, or at the very least the feeling of validation, I was receiving from these two men who I looked up to, coupled with the powerful sedative feeling that came from the heroin, had me hooked. For the next few years, heroin would be my drug of choice, although I was becoming increasingly more isolated when taking the drug, partly because it was very much frowned upon by my friends.

Remarkably, I managed to hold down a job as an apprentice greenkeeper, becoming fully qualified and ending up with a first assistant job at Gleddoch House near Port Glasgow. However, constantly being late and constantly coming in under the influence resulted in me being sacked. I was so scared to go home and tell my grandmother (who I was living with at the time) that I had lost my job, that when I got off the train at Paisley Gilmour Street Station and saw an Army recruiting wagon, I signed up there and then! As it turns out, joining the Army and giving your life for your country, was a far more desirable outcome than having to go home and face my grandmother with the news I had been sacked!

In the following three months, I managed to tidy my life up. I stopped using substances, got myself fit and was very soon away for Army training. I absolutely loved Army life. Everything about it just suited me and I was very quickly identified as being "switched on" which is Army jargon for someone who has potential and initiative. Within three months of arriving at my regiment, I was put forward for a promotion course and also joined the Reconnaissance or "Recce" Platoon. After doing a gruelling six week promotional course to earn my first stripe. I had been picked as being one of the top three finishers of the course. Forty men started and only eighteen finished. All of this was despite only being a class three private. You actually had to be a class one to get on the promotional course but I had managed to blag my way in, and was credited with showing initiative and "balls" by my superior officer! The night before I was due to march out on to the parade square and accept my award in front of friends and family, I got horribly drunk and woke up the following morning on the floor in a flat Edinburgh – this self-sabotaging behaviour was to become a staple in my life.

After a few years' service, I successfully completed several tours of Northern Ireland gaining a GSM (General Service Medal). I enjoyed the thrill of patrolling the streets of Northern Ireland. Unfortunately, I was injured in service during a riot in the fields of Drum Cree, Portadown, and subsequently diagnosed with PTSD resulting in an honourable medical discharge with a large pay-out and monthly pension. Being discharged devastated me and I returned home to the exact same area, people and temptations I had tried to escape from. I had a pocket full of money and a terrible attitude. I very quickly got involved in drug use once more.

Within a few months, I was chronically addicted to heroin and sedative tablets such as Valium and Temazepam. I had a reputation for being very extreme in terms of my drug use, almost as if I was on a mission to destroy myself. I started accumulating charges and was on the run from the police for a long time. I had been sectioned on a few occasions due to the deteriorating condition of my mental health. I was actually arrested, after the police came into the psychiatric hospital, where I was a patient at the time, on a drugs raid. Myself and another man had been bringing drugs and substances in, and distributing them amongst the patients. My life was absolute carnage. I ended up being sentenced to nineteen months in Barlinnie prison. Whilst in Barlinnie I was sent to the High Dependency Unit because of the concerns about my mental health. I was also constantly clashing with the officers, as I had very little respect for them. I was so arrogant it was unreal!

One day I was in my cell and an older, more experienced officer asked me if I'd like to go along to a Prison Fellowship group. At first I just declined but then he told me that it was a former prison officer, who was now retired, who was coming in to deliver the group. This intrigued me. "Why would an ex-prison officer want to come in here?" "What are these Christians all about?" I decided I would just go along to the group and wind them up a little bit. I actually stated at one point that I was in the group merely to disprove the existence of God! In the group, I was met by Derek Watt who was that former prison officer. Derek carried himself quietly but had the presence of a man much bigger than his physical stature. He had a quiet authority about him, but he also exuded a peace that was very intriguing. Derek was also very quick-witted, which helped us all warm to him and relax a little. In those groups we spoke openly about God, fellowship, the Bible etc. in a very sensible, normal way. It's fair to say I was utterly intrigued by all of this.

I attended the Prison Fellowship group every week diligently from that moment on, and I can honestly say that it was the highlight of my week. Although my attitude was not always great they always listened to what I had to say and gave me the time and space to express myself. Looking back now, I can see how quietly and skilfully the volunteers handled all I had to throw at them. I could also see very clearly that they had what I did not, peace.

One Tuesday morning I was sat in my cell with the door locked. I was on the bottom floor, four cells from the main entrance to the hall, my cell window overlooked the exercise yard. I could see the main gate. This day in particular it was raining, and volunteers were being escorted by a prison officer who had an umbrella as the weather was really bad. As they crossed the exercise yard during this really bad weather, I realised once again that here I was waiting at a window! I actually think I was waiting for them not to turn up so that I could say, "Well there you go, just like everyone else in my life." But every single week without fail, they just kept coming back. Eventually, it was that diligence and persistent show of compassion and commitment that won me round to the notion that God could, indeed, be real. I decided one night to pray for the first time, my logic being, whatever is driving these Prison Fellowship volunteers to come in week in week out, must be real, so that night I prayed. I remember opening my heart to God praying that He would show me that He was real. A simple ineloquent prayer, followed by real tears for the mess I had made of my life.

I woke up the next morning feeling very different internally and I believe at that moment, I was saved! However, on being released from prison, I very quickly fell into difficulties again. It was hard being a Christian on the outside. I had become addicted again and I was spiralling out of control. I reached out to Prison Fellowship and that evening, they helped find me accommodation in a Christian rehabilitation unit and my journey of change began. I was baptised in February 2003, with Derek Watt and the local pastor in the water with me. It was a special moment!

Over the past fifteen years I have managed homeless centres, rehabilitation units and been involved with many Christian charitable services. I have gained SVQ qualification, as well as an advanced care and management practice award, in Health and Social Care.

I have had my ups and down, as everyone has, but Prison Fellowship has been the constant anchor line in my life. Whenever life gets difficult, I simply tug on the rope, so to speak, and there they are! I am delighted to have been able to have worked for Prison Fellowship full time, using all my life experience as well as my work/management experience to help this amazing work continue. I can honestly say that

Prison Fellowship has, on numerous occasions, been nothing short of a lifesaver for me and I will be eternally grateful for Prison Fellowship and the people who have constantly gone the extra mile for me. I dread to think where my life would be had I not gone along to that meeting that morning in 2002, but all I can say is, I am glad I did!'

CHAPTER 11

Trustees' Voices

Prison Fellowship is served by a board of Trustees from a variety of backgrounds and experience including law, business, politics, finance, social work, chaplaincy, education and church. In this chapter, Ryan and Michael reflect on their faith and involvement with PFS. Ryan speaks from the perspective of someone who can empathise with the lifestyle and actions of many in prison, as well as their journey to faith. Michael is motivated by Jesus' call for justice, seeing advocacy and service as the outworking of faith.

Ryan Longmuir

'I am forty-two-years-old, married to Shirley-Ann for nearly twenty years, and have three lovely children. I have the real privilege of being a volunteer with PFS and more recently, being part of the Board of Trustees who oversee the charity. My own life experience has powerfully affected why I am so enthusiastic about my involvement with PFS.

When I was younger I made some bad choices and got involved with drug-taking. This gradually snowballed and I started to sell drugs. In 1999 my life had spiralled out of control and I wanted a change. I wanted to move away from Glasgow and the life I was living. I was scunnered with how my life had ended up. I decided at the age of twenty to take a year out and go to New Zealand. I left Scotland, but before I left, I decided to post over 100 Ecstasy tablets to the address I was going to be staying at in New Zealand. I arrived in NZ and a week or so later, the house I was staying in was busted by the police and the drug enforcement agency. I was arrested and taken into custody.

This situation became the catalyst for change in my life. I was given bail after spending a night in the local police office. Back in Scotland, I had a girlfriend who was someone I could confide in. After explaining the situation, she advised that I should pray. That evening before I went to bed, I remember getting down and kneeling – I thought that was how you prayed "God if you are real, show me that you are and I will believe in you. My life is a mess and I need your help". It made no difference. The following Saturday I was at a party high on drink and drugs, my life spiralling further out of control. On the Sunday morning, after being up all night partying, it was lashing with rain. On the way home I met two girls who were hitch-hiking, and praying that the next car would give them a lift to church. I stopped and asked where they were going, to which they replied, "We are going to church, would you like to come?" My response was a little colourful. I did not know many people in NZ and thought "What have I got to lose?" The church was held in a hotel. I was surprised when I walked in saw lots of young people and a band. My understanding of church was pews, old people and everyone in woolly jumpers.

That day was the start of me finding the God, who does exist and loves me, and sent His Son Jesus so that I could be forgiven and have a transformed life. I realised how fortunate I was to be still alive even though I was facing jail and had messed up big time. The girls asked me if I would like to pray with them. I was not 100 per cent there, but something happened. I saw that the drugs were just destroying my life and ruining all those around me. I threw the drugs I had in the ocean and have never taken drugs since. The girls said, "We want to help you get off drugs and really get to know Jesus". Their kindness allowed me to see that there was something in this Christianity thing. For the first time in my life, I acknowledged all the wrong things and sin that I had committed in my life. I know that Jesus died for me – I experienced it that night and have never been the same since. This was the start of an adventure that I am still on.

I continued to attend church, was reading the Bible and discovering this new life. While on bail I had to present every Monday and Friday at the police station. After seven months my court case arrived. All my new friends and many of my new church family, took a day off their work to come and support me at court. I had been at court many times before and would have had the odd friend or my Dad with me, but never so many people. I was told to expect two years in prison because of previous convictions, however, I was given a suspended sentence, deferred for twelve months, and community service.

I returned to Scotland as my Work Visa was revoked. My friends were amazed when they found out that I was now a radical for Jesus and not taking drugs anymore. This was the first time I connected with Prison Fellowship. I got the yellow phone book and called the number and spoke to Colin Cuthbert, who directed me to Cumbernauld Community Church – now Freedom City Church. It was a lively place and I just felt that was where I was meant to be. The church became a place that helped me grow in my faith. I met my wife in this church and was part of the leadership there for twenty years. I also connected with PFS to get involved in a prayer group in Glenmavis.

In 2003 an opportunity came to start my own business. I had this dream to create a business that I could give employment opportunities to those from troubled backgrounds. I was inspired by Jamie Oliver who had done this amazing thing called "Fifteen" – a restaurant in Cornwall where he employed troubled kids, and gave them skills that allowed them to have a career in hospitality. I was pretty full-on building my business and went to college to learn to cook. I did this for ten years.

After those ten years of growing my business, I felt a real desire to get back involved with prison work. A friend from church, Marc Pawson, who was a Christian rapper, was doing stuff in prisons and I asked could I come along and work with him. It was 2013. We visited prisons with Marc rapping and me sharing my story. I just loved this. We went to HMP Shotts round about this time doing a special concert during Prisoners' Week. I was invited by Keith and Anne Point, who lead the PFS group in Shotts, to come in and speak with the guys. I did this and loved it and was then asked to see if I would like to be a volunteer with PFS. I met up with Terry Paterson and became a registered volunteer. I had originally committed to go into Shotts every second week, but just loved it and before long was part of the PFS group going in every Monday night and have done this for the past six years.

I have had the privilege of being about and making friends with, some very wealthy people, although, my greatest joy and honour is being part of PFS' work with men in prison. I get so much more out of PFS than I put in. I have become friends with R. who is now near the end of a long sentence. On Christmas Day he called to wish me a Merry Christmas. It is these moments that make it all worthwhile – to see the hope that Jesus has brought. Every life is of the greatest value to Jesus. To be like Jesus looking after one lost sheep is the greatest endeavour we can be involved in. Seeing those written off by society finding hope in Jesus, never stops inspiring me. At an event in HMP Shotts, Kenneth McKenzie and his wife Angela were part of a worship service that was streamed live. Kenneth was introduced to me as the Chairman of PFS. He asked me to consider becoming a PFS Trustee. My wife and I were invited along to the PFS trustee meeting. We had a great time meeting some of the original founders of PFS who have faithfully been serving prisoners for forty years. It is a great joy and privilege to be part of PFS and I am looking forward to the next forty years.'

Michael Robinson

'As a child I grew up in Edinburgh, surrounded by a loving family, a comfortable lifestyle and a private education. I felt very blessed but always overcome with a sense of not living up to the opportunities God gave me; a guilt of falling short: "Why me? Why should I be the one who has everything I need?" As Christians, we are supposed to be transformed. Our lives should be different. It's not only clear in the Scriptures, but in the lives and examples of those Christians who have gone before us. I however, was comfortable and did not challenge myself to confront transformation. As I write this, I'm reminded of the words of Pope Benedict XVI: "The world offers you comfort, but you were not made for comfort. You were made for greatness!"

When I was eighteen, I reached a point in my life when I realised that either I could stop playing at being a Christian (having been raised in the faith), or I could live out my faith fully. I decided on the latter: "I want to love God and love others more. I want to be more like Jesus." I finally realised that God has made us to know Him, to love Him, and to serve Him in this world. It was also at this point, I decided to dedicate my professional life to standing up for, and providing a voice for, the forgotten and most vulnerable groups in society. For the past decade, after completing law school, I have been blessed to work with some incredible organisations and live out the promise I made. Whether it be by campaigning for children in care, advocating for refugees, or seeking equality for the unborn child, the common theme is justice.

When we look at the life of Jesus and the mandate given to us throughout Scripture, it is clear that Christ-followers are called to humbly and boldly reveal the just nature of Christ in our service to others. Indeed, every day, Christians pray for justice and mercy in the prayer that Jesus taught us: "Thy kingdom come, Thy will be done, on earth as it is in heaven." Every day, Christians recognise both that we are guilty of sin and that we are forgiven: "Forgive us our trespasses as we forgive those who trespass against us." This common and unifying prayer, the Lord's Prayer, recognises our failures and offences, and acknowledges our dependence on God's love and mercy.

It was my yearning for justice, and desire to build up the Kingdom of God, that led to my involvement with PFS. In January 2018 I was asked to become a Trustee. Being part of a global movement of people motivated by their faith to transform lives and communities by bringing love through action, acting with justice and showing mercy, is a blessing. On a more local note, and of relevance to PFS, the one thing that is apparent from the conversations I've had with my fellow trustees, our wonderful volunteers and the prisoners we serve, is the palpable and pivotal place prayer has in our mission at Prison Fellowship. Indeed, prayer is at the front and centre of all that we do, and where it all began in 1981.

Pope Francis recently reflected on the nature of the Christian faith: "We, the men and woman of the Church, are in the middle of a love story: each of us is a link in this chain of love." Prison Fellowship is a ministry, par excellence, of love and healing that fosters hope, dignity, and opportunities for new beginnings for prisoners and their families affected and often forgotten individuals by incarceration through the proclamation of the Good News of Jesus Christ.

A person's past does not have to dictate his future. Consider the apostle Paul, a former religious zealot, who had burned in his hatred for Christians and conspired in putting them to death for their faith. Yet Jesus called Saint Paul to Himself, directed him to write most of the New Testament, and arguably turned him into the Early Church's greatest missionary to the Gentiles.

For me, when I think and pray about PFS, I'm reminded of *Les Misérables* and not for the obvious criminal justice themes. The line: "To love another person is to see the face of God" encapsulates both why we exist, and how we operate as Christian disciples in prison ministry.

A Christian understanding of justice starts with the eternal in mind. It starts by seeing people as God sees them – recognising that we are all created in the image and likeness of God. A minister once taught me that "peace" is not just the absence of conflict, but the presence of justice. When we as a society recognise the inherent dignity of every human person and Christian justice, we will have a more peaceful world. Ultimately, Prison Fellowship, conversation by conversation, plays a significant, yet immeasurable part of that path.'

Chapter 12

What Next?

Y ou've heard the voices of a wide variety of people connected with our prisons in Scotland, ranging from prison governors and inspectors, to the men and women who have been convicted and some of whom are still serving time in prison. You've heard how, over the long history of Prison Fellowship Scotland, lives have been transformed as staff and volunteers have faithfully and passionately communicated the Gospel of Jesus.

From late 2019 on, the world faced unprecedented times, as the Covid 19 virus spread across every continent. Millions died and many more millions were ill, with many requiring intensive care. Slowly a programme of mass vaccination is thankfully helping society to return to what is being called a 'new normal'.

In October 2019, just months before the pandemic drastically curtailed our work, Prison Fellowship Scotland appointed a new Executive Director, John Nonhebel. Let's listen, as we hear from John and look ahead to all that God has in store for us.

John Nonhebel, Executive Director, Prison Fellowship Scotland

'I had the privilege of joining Prison Fellowship Scotland at the end of 2019 and was immediately struck by the huge privilege it is to work with the men and women in the prisons in Scotland. Although most of my working life had been in work among the poor and marginalised, I quickly realised how little I knew and is generally known, about the work that happens in prisons and I was keen to spend time visiting chaplains and understanding their work. I enjoyed seeing all the opportunities they have to reach out to vulnerable men and women, whether this was in the formal acts of worship, remembrance and celebration; in one-to-one meetings at the request of prisoners: or in facilitating the Prison Fellowship groups. It all helped me realise that as men and women find themselves in Scottish prisons because of poor choices they have made, it is not uncommon that God uses this time to get their attention and help them get started on a journey of knowing Him.

Joining Prison Fellowship at the time that I did has proved challenging and interesting. I had only been in post for about four months when the Covid-19 pandemic hit the country and as the country went into its first lockdown, so access to all the prisons in Scotland was stopped. Initially, we had hoped that it would only be for a short period of time but as we look to finalise the text for this book, it is now almost one year since these restrictions came into place, and in that time we have had only very limited access to two prisons, HMP Greenock and HMP Edinburgh, and even this has now stopped.

As I reflect on the pandemic it is important to recognise that the biggest challenge has been for the prison authorities to keep the men and women in prison safe. We are very grateful that there have no serious outbreaks of Covid-19. While sadly there have been a few deaths, these have been thankfully few. We also recognise how difficult it has been for those in prison, often locked up for more than twenty-two hours in the day, with very little or no access to education and other initiatives, and only a minimum amount of exercise allowed.

These restrictions have also brought challenges to us in Prison Fellowship Scotland, Very early on we realised that we would need to find new opportunities for people to find ways of connecting and being kept up to date with what was happening in the prisons, so that we could know how to pray. This led us to starting an online prayer meeting using the popular Zoom technology. This has proved to be a great success with twenty to thirty people meeting together every week. For many, it has become a fixed event in their diaries, and it has been a joy to see volunteers getting to know each other through this technology. We have also enjoyed having chaplains and people from partner organisations joining us for these online meetings and sharing with us key things for prayer. This has also been strengthened by our new monthly prayer diaries, with daily prayer points circulated to our supporter base and being made available as a downloadable resource on our new website.

Another way that we were able to respond to the restrictions brought on by Covid 19, was to partner with Junction 42 and Connect to Community, to provide a Christmas gift pack to approximately 7500 men and women in the Scottish prison system. This offer was taken up by fourteen out of the fifteen prisons in Scotland. The pack included a small chocolate bar, a craft item, a Christmas card and importantly, literature from the Scottish Bible society explaining more about the real meaning of Christmas – we had extremely positive feedback from the chaplains on these.

But as we look beyond the pandemic, what is in store for Prison Fellowship Scotland? From the beginning, our main focus has always been on helping the men and women in prison understand the Christian faith by exploring the Bible. We continue to have the opportunity to do this in the majority of the prisons in Scotland and I hope that some of the prisons, where we currently don't have this opportunity, would open up to us. In PFS we have many volunteers who have committed themselves to this ministry for a long time and have been faithfully serving in our prisons for many years. I hope that in the coming years we will recruit a new generation of volunteers to continue this work, learn from those that have been doing it for so many years, and help the men and women in our prisons discover a God who cares and loves them. I am also excited by the new letter-writing project which we are doing, and the opportunities this will give for a new group of volunteers to partner with us, and for them to be able to share something of their own faith in the letters they write.

The strapline for the Scottish Prison Service is "Unlocking potential and transforming lives". Sadly for many of those who end up in our prisons that is far from the reality, with many stuck in the revolving door of making poor choices, getting caught in criminal activity, being sent to prison and then on release ending up back in the same community and making the same choices – so much so that we have volunteers that have seen different generations of the same family going through the prison system. Through our Sycamore Tree course, which looks at the subject of restorative justice and victim awareness, we help men and women understand better the consequences of the crimes they have committed and realise that they can make different choices. There is a growing demand for this course to be delivered in our prisons and we are in process of building and training the team of volunteers who are able to deliver this.

We also really value the opportunities we have to work with the families of those in prison, both through helping facilitate adventure holidays for the children of families affected by imprisonment and also, through Angel Tree, helping men and women in prison have a gift to give to their children at Christmas.

These are all hugely important and significant activities which PF Scotland is already involved in, but we also need to ask the question, 'What else God has in store for us?' I think there are some important questions that can guide us.

- How do we help men and women in Scottish Prisons discover their true value in God's sight? How do we help them discover faith? How do we, as Luke chapter 4 says, become involved in setting the prisoner free, not in its most literal sense, but rather free to be the people God intended them to be; free to make good positive choices in life; and free to resist the temptation to get caught up in crime and addictive behaviour.

- How do we help men and women in jail, who are on a journey of faith, grow in their knowledge and understanding of God, and understand more of what the Bible has to say? How do we help them become beacons of light in the prisons where they are serving their sentence?

- What more can we do to help stop the revolving door of men and women constantly in and out of prison? How do we work more with organisations that are focussed on throughcare, helping prisoners get established back into the community and receiving support?

- How can we work with all churches and denominations across Scotland to make them aware of the opportunities to work with men and women in prison, and better understand their needs? How do we work to help ensure that when people in prison are out of sight, they are not out of our minds? How could we help establish a stronger prayer network across Scotland focussed on praying for all of those who are connected with the Scottish Prison service, whether they be prisoners or staff?

CHAPTER 13

Conclusion

That's the inside story of the 'Forty Years Behind Bars' of Prison Fellowship Scotland, from the perspectives of all the people with whom we come into contact. We hope you have enjoyed listening to these voices and found them informative.

You will have discovered, as you have read this book, and listened to the many voices, how much our work is needed and how rewarding and fulfilling it can be. You could be part of a team that goes into your local prison. You will be trained and mentored by PFS and by SPS chaplaincy.

You can join us for our regular weekly prayer meeting when volunteers from all over the country bring our work to God in prayer using Zoom. You could set up a support prayer group in your church or keep your church prayer meeting informed of the weekly work of PFS. Prayer underpins all our work.

You might not feel you can go into a prison but would be happy to write to someone who has no visits or outside contact. Again we would train and support you through the process.

You may be especially interested in the care for the children of men and women in prison and would help to raise funds to send a child on an SU holiday or make sure they have a gift from their parent at Christmas. We would love you to be partners with us in the privilege of serving men and women in prison and their families.

If you are interested in our work, to volunteer, to pray, to support or to know more, please take a look at our website: www.pfscotland. org or contact us via the website or:

Facebook page:https://www.facebook.com/Prison
FellowshipScotland/ or email office@pfscotland.org

HEAVEN,
HOW I GOT HERE

THE STORY OF THE THIEF ON THE CROSS

COLIN S. SMITH

Heaven, How I Got Here

The Story of the Thief on the Cross

Colin S. Smith

What if you woke up one morning knowing that it was your last day on earth? That's what happened to the thief on the cross, who died a few feet from Jesus. *Heaven, How I Got Here* is his story, told in his own words, as he looks back from Heaven on the day that changed his eternity, and the faith that can change yours.

I've never read anything like this! This compelling first-person account from a heavenly perspective helped me understand and appreciate what Jesus endured on the cross and why he did it.

Collin Hansen

Editorial Director, The Gospel Coalition and author of *Blind Spots*

Here is a gripping account of God's amazing grace that comes alive as recounted from this unusual and really helpful perspective.

Alistair Begg

Senior Pastor, Parkside Church, Chagrin Falls, Ohio

...brilliant idea beautifully executed...combines pastoral wisdom and narrative skill to help us get inside the heart and mind of the thief on the cross, crucified next to the Christ on Calvary.

Justin Taylor

Executive vice president, Crossway Books and blogger, 'Between Two Worlds', Wheaton, Illinois

978-1-7819-1558-5

Christian Focus Publications

Our mission statement —

STAYING FAITHFUL

In dependence upon God we seek to impact the world through literature faithful to His infallible Word, the Bible. Our aim is to ensure that the Lord Jesus Christ is presented as the only hope to obtain forgiveness of sin, live a useful life and look forward to heaven with Him.

Our books are published in four imprints:

CHRISTIAN
FOCUS

Popular works including biographies, commentaries, basic doctrine and Christian living.

CHRISTIAN
HERITAGE

Books representing some of the best material from the rich heritage of the church.

MENTOR

Books written at a level suitable for Bible College and seminary students, pastors, and other serious readers. The imprint includes commentaries, doctrinal studies, examination of current issues and church history.

CF4•K

Children's books for quality Bible teaching and for all age groups: Sunday school curriculum, puzzle and activity books; personal and family devotional titles, biographies and inspirational stories — because you are never too young to know Jesus!

Christian Focus Publications Ltd,
Geanies House, Fearn, Ross-shire,
IV20 1TW, Scotland, United Kingdom.
www.christianfocus.com
blog.christianfocus.com